APPLY THE LAWS IN THIS
SERIES AND EXPERIENCE

TRANSFIGURATION

Sister Thedra

Volume III

Copyright © 2021 by Halls of Light, LLC

All rights reserved. This book or any portion thereof may not be reproduced or used in any manner whatsoever without the express written permission of the publisher except for the use of brief quotations in a book review.

ISBN: 978-1-7366487-2-8

TRANSFIGURATION

A complete change of form or appearance into a more beautiful or spiritual state. "in this light the junk undergoes a transfiguration; it shines"

The transfiguration is a sign that Jesus was to fulfill the Law and the prophets. It also assured James, Peter, and John the Jesus was indeed the Messiah.

In Christian teachings, the Transfiguration is a pivotal moment, and the setting on the mountain is presented as the point where human nature meets God: the meeting place for the temporal and the eternal, with Jesus himself as the connecting point, acting as the bridge between heaven and earth.

To the Reader

Please read and review "Divine Explanations" on page 242 for questions and definitions of terms. This book is only a portion of the teachings and prophecies that have been given by Sananda (Jesus Christ), Sanat Kumara, and others of the higher realms, and Recorded by Sister Thedra.

Dedications

These volumes, entitled TRANSFIGURATION are dedicated to Sheryl McCartney and Kamalakar Durgapu, without whose invaluable assistance this work would not have been possible.

Contents

LORD OF HOST 1

FELLOWSHIP 31

NO TIME TO WASTE! 89

THAT WHICH I AM 155

THIS RESURRECTION 203

Mission Statement 235

Sananda's Appearance 236

About the Late Sister Thedra 237

Divine Explanations 242

Other Books by TNT Publishing 253

Esu Jesus Sananda

This reproduction is from an actual photograph taken on June 1st, 1961, in Chichen Itza, Yucatan, by one of thirty archaeologists working in the area at the time. Sananda appeared in visible, tangible body and permitted His photograph to be taken.

LORD OF HOST

"LORD OF HOST AM I, OH LORD OF HOST-- LORD GOD AM I: BLEST ART THEY WHICH ASK OF ME, FOR I AM THE LORD THY GOD, SENT THAT THERE BE LIGHT- I AM HE WHICH STANDS READY TO RECEIVE THEE UNTO MYSELF IN THAT DAY WHEN ALL MEN SHALL BE GATHERED UNTO ME.

LET IT BE KNOWN THAT ALL WHICH DOTH APPEAR TO BE MAN, ART NOT OF MANKIND: FOR IN THE BEGINNING GOD DID CREATE MAN: THEN ANOTHER DID SOURCE, AND HE DID ORDER ANOTHER LIKENESS, WHICH DID <u>APPEAR</u> TO EMULATE THE FIRST.

YET MINE CHILDREN, THE ONE WHICH FOLLOWED THE FIRST WAST COUNTERFEIT IT WAST <u>NOT</u> THE "IS-REAL" WHICH WAST NOT THE "IS-REAL-LIGHTS" WHY OH WHY, HAST THOU NOT FOUND THINE WAY HOME?

FOR THE REASON THOU HAST BEEN IN BONDAGE--- BOUND BY THE DARKNESS OF THE SECOND CREATION BY THE ONE CAST OUT.

WHILE I SAY UNTO THEE THERE HAST BEEN YET OTHER FORMS OTHER THAN THAT WHICH THOU HAST CALLED "MAN"-- I SAY: MAN HAST CREATED UNTO HIMSELF IN HIS UNKNOWING, IN HIS TIME OF IGNORANCE-- HE HAST CREATED "THINGS" WHICH HAST TORMENTED HIM-- YET IT IS BECAUSE THE SECOND CREATION BY AND OF THE ONE CAST OUT.

I AM NOW COME THAT THOU BE FREE FROM SUCH AS THE SECOND (CREATION) AND ALL THAT WHICH HAST FOLLOWED AFTER.

BE YE AS ONES PREPARED TO RECEIVE ME AND OF ME, FOR I HAVE GREAT THINGS TO REVEAL UNTO THEE.

I AM THE LORD OF HOSTS, SANANDA, SON OF THE MOST HIGH LIVING GOD SOLEN AUM SOLEN

Sweet is the Honey

Sweet is the honey from Mine mouth- for it shall be as the honey unto thine stomach, it shall nourish thee in the time of famine and it shall soothe thine wounds and bind them up- for it shall be sweet unto thee, blest art they which doth partake of the honey which I give unto thee for they shall be as the inheritors of Mine kingdom- let them taste of the sweetness thereof and be as ones prepared for the greater part, for therein is wisdom.

Mine time is now come when I shall step forth as one in flesh and bone and I shall touch them which have partaken of the honey, so be it they shall be blest this day- Hear ye that which I say unto thee and be ye blest- forever blest, for I Am the Lord thy God, Sananda. I Thedra, had seen in spirit a large man in a dress suit, coat lighter than the pants, he had been eating honey, it had dripped over his clothing, much as the rosin, or pitch would drip from the pine, or spruce tree. I called his attention to it.

Recorded by Thedra

Holy Ordinances

Justice be Mine in all things- for I Am Justice- I Am Love- I Am Peace- I Am thine Father, I Am the Son- I Am the Holy Parent from which cometh thou-

I Am the church- thou art the members - thereof - while I say unto thee the church is the holy body of Christ made up of Mine children which obey the laws which I give unto them- the holy ordinance which I have unfolded unto them- I say <u>Mine</u> <u>Ordinance</u> shall be kept holy- held within thine heart for I am the giver of the holy ordinances and these <u>Mine</u> ordinances shall be unto thee <u>Mine</u> <u>Word</u>, Mine commandments by which thou livest and return unto Me- for this have I given them unto thee-

Now ye shall set straight thine house- and clean out all old concepts- precepts- all the chaff, the pollution, corruption which hast been stored therein- ye shall no longer put thine foot into the filthy places of corruption wherein they put their Saints to death - wherein they give unto their fellow man the bitter cup- wherein they partake of the carcass- wherein they do defile the temple: wherein they drink of the pollution of the <u>wine</u>- I say unto thee ye shall come to know the meaning of the "Wine" the "<u>Holy Sacrament</u>"-

Ye shall prepare thine ownself for to receive of the "Holy Sacrament" for none other shall partake- I say unto thee the "Holy Sacrament" shall not touch the lips of the ones which are unprepared- for this have I said: "cleanse thine own temple" then ye shall partake of the fullness of Mine house- blest are they which partake thereof for I am the fullness- I Am the All---

While I say unto thee thou art Mine children, I say ye have been long away- NOW ye shall prepare thine self for thine return unto Me and ye shall go out no more for I bid thee return unto Me-

For this do I say unto thee put thine house in order- bless thineself by thine own works- purify thine self as ye would that I purify thee- for I bid thee arise- shake off thine legirons- be ye no part of their wanton- their foolishness- be ye aware of every word which goeth from thine lips for it is life which thou givest unto it; by Mine grace have I endowed thee with the power of speech- use it to bless thine own self- for have I not blessed thee accordingly- I say ye shall walk humbly and gently among men, and ye shall bless them by every word which proceeds from thine mouth- be ye as ones which have ears to hear that which I say unto thee and let it bless thee for I am thine Eternal Parent- .

Solen Aum Solen

Recorded by Thedra

I am Limitless

Beloved children: While I do speak unto thee in thine own language- I say unto thee, I am not limited by word of mouth, by language for I know not limitation- I am the all of creation, I have created all which is eternal within thine world: which shall endure forever-

Now while I speak in words which thou hast been familiar with, I say, I am limitless- and words of thine language is not sufficient to convey unto thee the fullness of Mineself- neither Mine work: for it is the lesser part which thou dost see or understand-

<u>Yet</u> I tell thee of greater things in the hours of thine sleep- while I say unto thee thou art <u>not</u> bound by the form, I say thou art free from all limitations as eternal beings, for thou art not of the nether kingdom- thou art of Mine kingdom born of Me- eternal beings-.

Now--- ye shall accept thine inheritance- willed unto thee of Me from the beginning-

Mine children I have spoken unto thee of Mine self- Mine life- which I Am- I say thou art one with Me, accept Mine holy word- be ye blest thereby and be ye glad forever more- for I say unto thee great is thine inheritance.

I Am that I Am-

Solen Aum Solen.

Sweet is the Living Word

Sweet are the words of the living God- sweet are the words of Him which cometh as on wings of the morn- by the living word shall ye be made new- by the living word shall ye be delivered out- by the living shall ye be made whole-

By the living word shall the veil be parted-

By the living word shall ye be made to see.

By the living word shall ye return unto thine abiding place.

By the <u>LIVING</u> word shall ye come into the place wherein I am- So shall it be, for I am that I AM.

Solen Aum Solen

Recorded by Thedra

The Key

By Mine mouth hast the word been spoken which shall be unto thee thine Shibboleth and thine Shield- I have given unto thee the "Key" which shall open up the door of the inner temple-

While I say unto thee there are many which hast received the "Key" they know not the power of it- its great part- I say unto thee it is the "Secret of Secrets"- it is the <u>greatest</u> of all <u>tools</u>- it is the "Key" unto their victory- yet they know <u>not</u> <u>peace</u>-- they have not turned the Key- they have hidden it within the rubbish of their thinking- midst their <u>opinions</u>- their preconceived ideas; and opinions- while I say they shall bring it out and find its proper place and place it carefully within the lock: then the door shall swing wide that they might enter into the Holy of Holies-.

So be it the Way

I Am Sananda

The Word

Behold! The works which I do- see the word made manifest- for I say unto thee the word hast gone out from Mine mouth which shall become manifest in thine word of form, watch, see, behold- for I the Lord thy God hast spoken!!

Let not the words of thine mouth betray thee*- for I say unto thee the words of thine mouth shall be praise unto the Father Solen Aum Solen- and unto Him all the glory- glorify His name- and be ye as ones prepared for the greater part-

Let His name ring within thine heart--

Be ye as ones filled with joy- harken ye unto that which I say for I Am The Lord thy God

Sananda

Recorded by Thedra

* No negative talk.

I Did Say: I Shall Return

Behold- I am come, the one which hast awaited this day- when I might walk among them which hast kept their covenant with Me- I say unto them I am come that Mine part might be fulfilled- I say unto them I come that ye might go where I go-

Now! it is come when I have returned unto thee for the purpose of fulfilling Mine promise- Mine covenant- that it might be finished <u>this day</u>- never wast it finished- for I did say: "I shall return unto thee that where I go ye might go also"- So let it be-

For this do I say unto thee: be ye about thine preparation that it might be so- So let it be as the <u>Father</u> <u>hast</u> <u>Willed</u> it. I come that His will be done in Me- through Me and by Me- this <u>day</u>- so let it be- I say unto thee let it be done! For I am come unto thee that it be done as He hast sent Me for that purpose- call unto them which hast ears to hear- and say unto them as I would say- that "He is come that where He goes ye might go also" So let them hear that which I say <u>this</u> <u>day</u>- be it the truth and the light by which they shall come-

I give unto thee of Mineself that they might come to know Me- So be it they that have ears <u>to</u> <u>hear</u> shall know Mine voice and respond unto it-

Let thine light so shine that they Might follow it-

So be it I am the Lord thy God

Sananda

Recorded by Thedra

Joy of Serving

Blest be this day- while I say unto thee "blest be this day"- I say ye too shall be blest- bless thine own self as ye would be blest of Me- for have

I not said ye are Mine hands- Mine feet made manifest- have I not given unto thee a part which ye shall do with joy and gladness? I say unto thee ye shall serve Me with joy and gladness- let all thine serving be with gladness and joy- for this is thine part- thine joy is thine reward- hear ye that which I say and be ye blest- for have I asked of thee aught? Have I not given of Mineself that ye be blest?

Have I not found Mine reward in the joy of serving? while I say unto thee follow ye Me- shall ye not learn of Me- that ye might go where I go--? While I say unto thee bless thine self as ye would that I bless thee- I say that I shall bless thee according unto thine labor- I am not unmindful of Mine servants- have I forgotten them? Nay! Mine children- nay- never wast it so! never shall it be- for I am a mindful God- which hast watched over thee in the hours of thine unknowing--

While thou hast not remembered Me and Mine mercy I have cared and provided for thee as the suckling infant- yet it is now time that ye arise and take upon thineself thine own sonship and be responsible for thineself and for thine part- waste not thine substance on the wonton ones who ask not of Me- be ye as ones watchful for Mine sheep which hungereth and thirsteth for Mine word- which shall feed them, these are thine responsibility- seek out them which seek Me out- which doth ask of Me- and therein is wisdom- bless thineself in the doing- for this do I counsel thee thusly-

I Am Sananda

Son of God

Recorded by Thedra

Communication

The time is come when ye shall come to know Me, thy Brother known as Pash- and it shall be for the good of all- for I say unto thee it shall be for the benefit of all mankind this communion of ours.

Now it cometh when I shall speak forth in the name of our Father which hast sent Me for this My part- let it be understood that I come with and by the consent of the Great White Brotherhood- and it is through the mercy and love of our Father that it is made possible- for He hast given us the wisdom and the power of communication one with the other- let it be unto His glory- for this do I speak out this day-

Now ye shall come unto this altar at the evening time for a word which I shall give unto thee- I bless thee with My presence as ye shall bless them which doth come into thine presence- So be it that they shall be blest of Me through thee- I Am thine older Brother -

The Word is Not Yet Understood

Now Mine beloved ones the time is come when one shall give unto thee a part which shall be for the good of all- at this time it is expedient that He speak- I say it is expedient that He speak unto thee that they might come to know that which He has to say- while the word hast been given it is for the greater part yet not understood by the uninitiated- while I say the word hast been given for them which have ears to hear and a mind to learn- they as yet have not comprehended the fullness of the word- ye shall now receive this One as a Brother and as one illumined of God the Father- Be ye so blest- I Am Sananda---

Wait for no man, ask of no man his part, his worth shall be proven by his deeds, by the giving of himself that others be lifted up- it is said that it is the greater blessing to give than to receive: to ask for others than thine self- while a man proves his worth by his giving of himself he doth work for the good of all, asking nought save the joy of giving- Be he where ever he be- what ever he be it is not hidden from the all seeing eye*-

He is revealed unto Him that which he is, and nothing is hidden- wherein is there a hiding place? I ask; wherein is there a hiding place?

So long as he waits for another he stands still- moves neither forward nor backward- yet others pass him by- will it not profit him to go forward? I say the one which goes forward moves of his own will, and under his own momentum- when one asks of another he hast deprived that one his own will- for he has but to be alert unto the need at hand and do that which is to be done- ask of another how ye might serve him- yet ask him not to serve thee- for therein is servitude- and not fellowship- be ye as ones blest to serve each other in the name of the Father, Son and Holy Ghost- So let it be for the good of all mankind-

Now while I say unto thee ye bless thyself in the serving others- so let it be- for this do I come that I might serve thee- ask of Me and I shall do that which ye ask in the name of our Father which hast sent Me- So be it My joy to serve thee-

Be ye blest as I have been blest-- I am at thine Service- I Am-

*He, the all-seeing eye: God

Recorded by Thedra

Accept This Day

Beloved of Mine being- it is now come when one shall speak unto thee for the sake of them which know not- while I say unto thee it is for their sake- I too say it is for the good of all mankind- hear Him and that which He says unto them- for it shall be given unto thee for them-

Bless thineself in the giving for it shall be given as it is received- no word shall be changed- I am thine older Brother and Sibor Sanat Kumara-.

Beloved it is now come when I shall give unto thee a part for them which know not- it is for all which have ears to hear, so let them hear that which I say-.

While it is given unto man to weary of the physical part which he hast chosen- he calls out for deliverance from that which he hast chosen- he cries out for surcease from his cares and misery- yet he hast waited for this day which is now come that he might be free from their woe- so I say unto them "Accept this day" with great joy and thanksgiving!

Let thine heart overflow with joy and thanksgiving for it is now come when the Lord thy God walks amongst thee- as for the greater part unknown- unsung- and without recognition, His only reward is thine love, obedience, and thine fellowship- so be it that He is now come that His people might be found and brought out before the great day of sorrows- I say unto thee 'that day' no man knows- but come it shall! While it is now come that He walks amongst thee unknown- He is one with the Father never the less for taking unto Himself flesh and bone- it binds Him not- while He is ever present, all powerful, all knowing, He is indeed in flesh at this moment- bound <u>NOT</u> by the laws of Earth, neither by any law!

While it is said He is The "Wayshower" He hast gone before thee to prepare the way for them which choose the way to the Fathers house- I too say ye follow of thine own free will and by thine own effort- thine own momentum- for none shall carry thee on their back- ye <u>walk</u> in the way set before thee- the "Key" hast been given unto thee- ye turn it with thine own effort-

Now ye shall be <u>mindful</u> of the "Word" of the living God- for I say unto thee He <u>liveth</u>- and He hast spoken unto thee <u>this</u> day that ye might know what He hast come to do- for this do I come that ye might be reminded of His part, His mission is clearly stated within these scripts and it is for thine own benefit that I say unto thee study them well! find the treasures buried therein- waste not thine opportunity- for it is a divine ordinance given unto thee for this day- it is with great joy that the doors of the Celestial Kingdom be opened unto thee <u>this</u> <u>day</u> when we might speak unto thee in thine own language- in thine own tongue- hear ye Me and give thanks this day- for the law is: that by the giving of thine own self- so ye bless thine own self- so let it be-

I have spoken that ye be blest, so accept it in the name of the Father which hast sent Me- I AM

Recorded by Thedra

Not by Supplication but Application

While I come that there might be light amongst thee- I say it is as a great call hast gone forth that all might hear- and it is not given unto Me to separate the sheep from the goats- yet I know them for that which they are- they hide not from Me- for I see them by their own light and they which are the chosen shall be brought out and given parts which shall prepare them for the greater part- while it is by their own light that they are found it is by their own actions, their own will and momentum that they come- the way is opened up- the call is out- the time propitious and the Sibors stand by in readiness- they extend a hand unto them which have chosen to accept it- so be it that this is the day- this is the hour in which to choose which way ye go-

Now let it be said that it is not by thine supplication that ye return unto the Fathers house- but by application of the law- the becoming as a little child- and ask of no man the way- ask of no man his opinion- his favor or his grace- for it is by the grace of our Father which hast sent Me that ye return unto his place of abode- so be it that He hast sent Me that I might bless thee as I have been blest- so let it be as he hast willed it-.

I Am thine older brother and thine Sibor

Sori Sori- Holy Holy is the day- blest art thou this day- rest thine head in the hollow of Mine hand this night and I shall bless thee for this do I speak unto thee from out the fullness of Mine love-

I Am Sananda

Recorded by Thedra

The Two Orders

Mine children the day approaches when all men shall stand with heads bowed in reverence of the Father which hast sent Me- I say unto thee- the Father hast given unto us life, unto us of Himself that we might be- So let it be that all "men" might come to know Him- I say unto thee "All Men" shall come to know Him- for this do we the Sons of God speak out this day- It is now come when the ones of perdition shall be exposed for that which they are- they shall no longer hold sway over the children of the most high living God- for I come that they be free from bondage- I say unto thee be ye as ones freed from all bondage- hasten ye to proclaim the truth unto them- they, the children of God the Father shall know no fear for I say unto them be ye as ones blest this day for I am come that ye be delivered up- Know ye that I am the Lord thy God sent of Mine Father- which is not of the Earth- neither the realms of darkness- that ye be delivered out- be ye as ones which have ears to hear and a mind to learn- I say hear ye Me and comprehend that which I say unto thee-

For there are many amongst thee which are not of Mine fold- I say many are amongst thee which are not of Mine fold- so let it suffice that I am with thee this day- seek ye the light and it shall not be hidden from thee-

So let thine own light so shine that all night see it-

I Am the Lord thy God

Sananda

Son of the Most High Living God-

Thou art this day commanded.- Be ye at peace and poise, behold the hand work of the Lord thy God: See that which He does, Behold! the time is now come when ye shall do His work that which is given unto thee to do- rest not on thine laurels, say unto them "He is come" "Behold the Lord is come!" He is with us in truth, and it is given unto Me to know Him for I am with Him in truth and in spirit- I say unto them- arise from thine slumbers- shake off the shackles, be ye up and about the work at hand, for ye shall do the part which is given unto thee to do with joy, and thanksgiving- blest are they which do give thanks for His coming- I say: "HE IS COME!" Let thine praise ring out through the cosmos it is now come when he walks amongst thee- hear ye Me and praise ye the name of Solen Aum Solen- The most high living God which hast sent Him-.

I Am Pash

Recorded by Thedra

Thine Faith Shall Be Justified

Mighty! O, Mighty is the Arm of The Lord thy God-!

I say unto thee Mighty! Is the arm of the Lord thy God!

Be ye swift to say unto them He is come- for it is nigh unto the time when they shall cry out for mercy and they shall find themself in great stress! I say unto thee be ye swift to say unto them "He is Come" Be ye as ones glad! for this do I say rejoice it is so- for I declare unto thee that it is so-

Wast it not said that He would return as a thief in the night to find them sleeping- I say it is done- Have "they" awakened unto His presence? Nay I say unto thee He is come- now "they" sleepeth still. While I say "they" sleepeth still I speak of them which deny him- "they" which await the signs and know not it is now time! I say the time is come when He shall give unto them the water of life- the bread for which they have asked-

<u>Now</u> I speak unto thee of them which have held steadfast and them which have prepared them self for <u>this</u> day- I say unto them it is come when thine faith shall be justified- so be it I speak unto thee Mine beloved- that they might know that which I say- I am come that ye be so blest of Me and by Me--

I Am Pash

Recorded by Thedra

Commandment of the Lord Sananda

Mine hand is extended unto all which have the will to accept it- and that which it holds for them- wast it not for the great stress which is to come upon them I should not extend it unto them which have not prepared themself- I say I would not extend Mine hand unto all at this time. Yet in Mine endeavor to lessen their stress I shall give of Mine self that they might have peace-

I say unto thee I bring <u>NOT</u> peace- I come that <u>they</u> <u>might</u> find peace- yet they give of themself that war and strife might continue- I say unto thee thine time shall be devoted unto peace- and unto Mine work for this have I called thee out from among them- I say unto thee- be ye at peace and poise- praise ye the name of Solen Aum Solen- give of thine self that others have peace- divide not thine self- give all thine self unto the service of the Lord thy God- for I say unto thee thine hands shall be Mine hands- thine mind shall be Mine mind- rest not on thine laurels- grieve not for them which have not the mind to follow Me- grieve not for them which betray themself- grieve not for the wonton- for I say unto thee be ye up and about the Fathers business- I say unto thee follow ye Me- and be ye glad-

I Am Sananda

Two Creations

Mine time shall be thine time- Mine hand shall be thine hand- ye shall walk in Mine footsteps- ye shall be as ones prepared for that which I give unto thee to do- ye shall give freely of thine time unto Mine work- for the whole of the plan no man knows which has not received of his inheritance in full- I say unto thee no man knows the fullness of the great and divine plan which has not received of his inheritance- for this do I say unto thee be ye up and about the Fathers business- for I have great things in store for thee-

While I speak unto thee it is for the good of all mankind and for that matter there are many which doth appear to be like unto man which are of another order- another specie- which are not of Mine fold- I say unto thee these are not of the Father born, they are not of Mine house- these are not of Mine fold- I say unto thee these are not created of Mine Father- therefore they are not capable of eternal life- be ye as ones enlightened- for I speak unto thee that it be so- so let it be- I have spoken and thou hast heard Me- I say I have spoken unto all which are of a mind to hear and be enlightened of Me for I am the Lord thy God- come that it be so-

I Am that I Am

Sananda

Recorded by Thedra

Thus Sayeth the Lord of Hosts

Which hast been with thee this day shall be blest of Me and by Me- for I say unto thee they shall be blest for that which they do- that which they have done- that which they shall do- for I say unto thee they which come into the house of the Lord shall be blest- blest are they which give of themself that others be blest- So let it be- I say unto thee be ye as ones blest of Me- for have I set this Mine house up- upon a rock- the rock which I Am- I say unto thee I have founded this Mine house- I have brought it forth- I shall finish that which I have set into motion and it shall serve its purpose- and too I say unto thee I shall finish Mine mission and depart unto yet unknown realms- for I say unto thee there are realms yet unknown unto thee- for this have I said unto thee: "follow ye Me" that where I go ye might go also- so let it be-

I say unto thee be ye faithful in little things and I shall give into thine keeping greater things than thou hast imaged- be ye as ones alert and hasten to say unto them "He is come this day" for this do I say unto thee be ye alert and prepared to do Mine work- for art thou not Mine hands, Mine feet, Mine voice unto them- have I not made of thee Mine hand maiden, Mine voice that they might have knowledge of Me the Lord thy God- Be ye as one fore told of the greater things to be done-

I Am The Wayshower- I go before thee that ye might follow Me- so let it be as the Father hast willed it.

I am the one sent that it be so.

Sananda

Mighty, Oh Mighty art thou O' Father, Mighty is thine power, thine love hast brought us forth, thine hand hast sustained us, thine arm hast held us fast in the wandering to and fro, in the going and the coming- Oh Father wast it not for thine love we would not be- such is thine love that thou hast given of thine self that we might be immortal beings- We praise thee Father for thine love, for thine loving care, Oh Father take these thine children unto thine bosom and give unto them as thou hast given unto Me- I ask for them as I would ask for Mine self- Oh Father I thank thee thou hast heard us thine Sons- praise unto thee forever-

I Am Thine Son

Sananda

Recorded by Thedra

The Host Speaks

Mine beloved ones- while it is now come that others shall come into this for the purpose of giving unto thee assistance, I say they shall bless themself in the doing- for have I not said that I am the host in this house, have I not said unto thee serve Me with all thine heart, thine hands, thine will, for I say unto thee I accept no less- for this do I say serve Me diligently- serve me with thine whole heart!

Now I say unto them which cometh- serve me diligently, serve Me with a glad heart- and know ye that I am the Lord thy God- such is Mine word unto them which shall come into this house- I am the Lord thy God which hast brought it forth- So let it suffice-

I Am Sananda

Thine Whole Heart

Blessed ones- there are times when I speak unto thee in voices unheard by human ear, for ear hast not heard that which I speak unto the hearts of men- I say unto thee the heart of man is that with which we thine Sibors are concerned- I say unto thee open ye up thine heart and I shall abide therein, for have I not asked of thee thine whole heart? thine hand and thine feet shall be swift to do Mine bidding, thine light shall so shine that all might see it and know that I abide within thine heart- I speak unto them which are of Mine fold, for I say that none other shall abide with Me- for these which have a mind to follow Me shall come to know Me- they shall hear Mine voice and follow it, they shall keep the law with and by which I attained Mine freedom from the Earth and her bondage- I say I ask of thee nought save obedience unto the same law which is given unto us that we might attain-- and attain we have, therefore we now offer unto thee our hand- our heart- We extend unto thee a hand- ye have but to accept it in the name of the Father, Son and

Holy Spirit- I say unto thee there is no place wherein ye can be, wherein ye can not be found- for I am the Lord thy God- So be it I Am the Son of the most high living God-

I Am Sananda

So let it suffice that I am come that ye have light- I Am that I Am-

Mine children there many which have no peace- they cry out for mercy yet I say unto them be still and know that I am the Lord thy God and they hear not that which I say unto them- be ye at peace- let thine light shine that they might see it from afar- be ye blest as I have been blest- I bless thee with Mine light, Mine presence- has it not been apparent unto thee- I am present, I am ever with thee, be ye aware of Me- of Mine presence- and I shall lead thee every step of the way-

I Am that I Am

Recorded by Thedra

A Living Substance

Mighty, O Mighty is He the Lord thy God- Mighty, O Mighty are His words, for they shall be as the waters which shall give succor unto the dry and parched deserts - they shall be as the blood which gives life unto the physical bodies- long drained of their substance- I say unto thee the word of God shall become a living substance- a living substance, a thing tangible- for I say unto thee I speak the word and it becomes that which I decree-

Now Mine beloved ones I say unto thee ye shall come to know the meaning of the "word"- the power of the word - ye shall come to know the power invested within the "word" for I say I shall reveal unto thee many things which have <u>as</u> yet not been revealed unto thee- I say unto thee that I am the Lord thy God- and I am mindful of all thine cares and woes-

I say ye shall come unto Me un-opinionated, unseen by man- not for the eyes of men but in humility and with thanksgiving and I shall give unto thee as ye have not received- for it is now come when there shall be a great awakening, and many shall raise up and ask for light and they shall come inquiring of thee- and I say unto thee ye shall be as ones prepared to tell them- for I say unto thee it is now come when ye shall be as ones enlightened of Me and by Me- for do I not know thee and thine source? I say be ye aware of Me- and of Mine source, for this do I now speak unto thee that it be so-

So let it be.

I Am the Lord thy God-

Sananda

Recorded by Thedra

I Shall Do a Mighty Work

Behold! See the hand of the Lord thy God move- I say unto thee behold and see that which I shall do- for I shall do a mighty work, I shall perform a work wonderous to behold- for I am the Lord thy God- sent

forth from realms of great light- light such as Earth hast not yet known. while I say unto thee I am sent forth from realms of great light- I say I am sent forth from the source of all light which the Earth has as yet not known- for I say unto thee the finite hast not beheld the glory of the infinite for it is as yet not able to comprehend the fullness of such glory-

Yet I say unto thee the Earth is an ensouled being Divine in its origin- and hast been given unto man for his progress for his own sake- yet he hast misused- abused- and misused the energy which hast been allotted unto him, he hast betrayed himself and his trust--.

Now I say unto thee Mine beloved children hear ye that which I say and give unto Me credit for knowing that which I say, for I speak unto thee that ye might be prepared for the greater part- I say the greater part which is thine divine inheritance in full- for it is the Fathers will that ye be free- free from all bondage- forever free- I say <u>free</u> from <u>all</u> bondage-

Now it is come when ye shall go forth declaring the <u>truth</u> which shall make <u>them</u> free- be ye fearless in thine effort- be ye as a lamp unto their feet- walk ye in the way in which I lead thee- bless thine self in the doing and ask of no man his opinion for I am The Wayshower, I say unto thee "follow ye Me", and I shall lead thee out of bondage, long hast thou wandered in darkness--.

I say unto thee be ye as ones prepared for the greater things than thou hast imaged-

Let thine hearts be glad- thine feet be swift- thine hands be as Mine hands- be ye as Mine hand- for I say ye shall do Mine work and rejoice in the doing- for I am come that I might find Mine own- Mine own shall know Mine voice and follow it-

Let it be so-

I Am Sananda

Recorded by Thedra

I Shall Touch Thee

Behold the light shineth from the source of thine being! Behold the glory of this new day- be ye as ones blest to see- and to know that I am the Lord thy God- While I say unto thee behold the glory of the Lord thy God- I say unto thee "unto the Father all the Glory"- for this do I say unto thee behold the light which shineth from the source of thine being-

Now I say unto thee thine eyes hast not beheld such glory as they shall see- for it is given unto Me to know and I say unto thee thine eyes of mortal could not bear such glory as is His- I say unto thee the light which He bringeth shall blind them which are not prepared to look upon it- I say be ye as ones prepared for it is now come when I shall show Mine self in all Mine glory! For this do I say prepare thineself- I say unto thee-

Behold the Light which I Am-

See that which I shall do-

For I shall quicken thee and ye shall stand in wonderment at that which ye shall see- for I shall touch thee that ye might see- so let it be as the Father hast willed it-

I Am the Lord thy God

Sananda

Things Divine

Mine beloved ones: Have I not said unto thee many times thou art sons of God the Father- born of Him from out the source of all light wherein there is no darkness- I speak unto thee of things divine- for this do I come in spirit and truth that ye might have the truth- be ye as ones blest of Me and by Me- Now ye shall know that thou art holy in thine own right in thine own origin- ye shall give unto thine own self credit for being sons of God- ye shall walk which way thine crown tilts not- waver not- for I say unto thee ye shall stand firm- ye shall be as "the Rock" which I Am- ye shall be as the foundation upon which I shall build great and strong- ye shall be as the guardians of truth and justice- and ye shall not compromise for I say unto thee ye shall do that which I give unto thee to do with gladness within thine heart- ye shall be as guardians of Mine words- and as custodians of Mine wares- for I say unto thee I shall place within thine hands the instruments to do Mine work- ye shall not want- ye shall not need- for I the Lord God hast spoken unto thee of the <u>greater</u> part- and I shall see it through- be ye as ones prepared- so be it I Am-- and

I am the Lord thy God

Sananda

Recorded by Thedra

For the Acceptance

Beloved children- while I say unto thee it is time that ye arise and accept thine inheritance which is willed unto thee of the Father Solen Aum Solen- I too say it is thine now- "for the acceptance"- it is not spent- thine <u>fortune</u> is <u>intact</u>- it is given unto Me to know for I am the Lord thy God- I am the son of the Most high living God and I know that which is willed unto thee- I say- I have received Mine inheritance in full- be ye as I and wander no more in bondage- for it is thine inheritance to be free- let nothing be unto thee a <u>stumbling</u> <u>block</u>- for I say it is thine divine inheritance to be free- yet ye are bound by the law of Earth-

I tell thee ye shall be unbound and ye shall go and come freely- while thou hast not comprehended the freedom which shall be thine for the acceptance- ye shall accept it - it comes unto thee as a divine gift of Mine Father- I am the one which shall touch thee and I shall place upon thine head a seal which shall give unto thee power to go and to come as ye would- for I say unto thee the seal which I shall place upon thine forehead shall be unto thee power to loose thine legirons- to loose thine self from the gravitation of the Earth- and to go where ye would-

Now for this: do I say hear ye what I say unto thee- ye are born of God the Father- ye are one with Him- ye are eternal beings- blest of Him- ye are of the first generation- ye are of the sons of IsReal- oh mighty ones of IsReal hear ye that which I say unto thee- and arise, come forth and be ye as ones come alive- I am come that it be so- I Am

Sananda

The House of Isreal

Mighty, O, Mighty Sons of Is Real (Isreal) be as ones prepared to receive of Me that which I have kept for thee- for I say unto thee it is a princely fortune that I have kept for thee in the days of thine wanderings- and in the time of thine un-knowing- I say unto thee I have kept for thee thine fortune- and ye shall claim it and be as the sons of God which thou art-

I say unto thee Mine children thou art of the house of God thine Father- of the house of Isreal- and thou art now fortuned to be as one wandering in bondage; yet for this have I sent Mine son unto thee that thine wandering might end- let it be so- for I have so willed it- let it be- for this do I say unto thee be ye as ones prepared- for great shall be thine joy when ye have returned unto thine rightful estate- thine inheritance- I say unto thee O Mine sons- be ye blest of Me and by Me for I Am thy Father Eternal--

Solen Aum Solen

Recorded by Thedra

Sananda's Supplication

Most Holy Almighty Father bless these thine children as I have been blest- give unto them as thou hast given unto Me, Oh Father I thine Son Sananda ask for them that they might know that I thine Son know them and their needs, that thou art the Father Eternal, that thou art, that they have a place prepared where they might know peace such as they have not had in the time of their wanderings-

I ask of them nothing except obedience unto the law- open up their ears oh, Father, touch their eyes that they might see the glory of the Lord- such is Mine love for them that I give of Mine self that they might receive their freedom from bondage even as I- bless them Father with thine being, let them know as I know that thou art the cause of their being- rest their weary bodies that they might be as ones refreshed of Spirit- Father most gracious be unto them that which they have not known, the source of their being* Unto thee all the glory and all the praise-

I Am thine Son Sananda

*Here He is <u>not</u> <u>asking</u> but giving credit- accepting the truth, (fact)

Thedra.

Commandments

Be ye as Mine hand made manifest unto them and say unto them as I would that the time is now come when there shall be great stress upon the Earth, and amongst men- for nations shall be torn asunder and the heads of nations shall be brought low- thrones shall be overthrown and there shall be much weeping- for I say unto thee there shall be great changes upon the Earth and amongst the world of men- I say within the time which is near the great nations of the Earth shall sit about the council tables seeking peace- while they shall find none- for they have set into motion the misused energy which shall spend itself before there shall be peace.

I say unto thee be ye as one peaceful- let peace be within thine heart- put aside thine instruments of destruction and be ye blest in the doing- for I speak unto thee as the Lord thy God- which I Am- and I am not so foolish as to be part of thine foolishness- I say unto them I am not part of their foolishness- I give not of Mine time or energy unto their wars and strife- I bless not the aggressor- I hear not his prayers- I give not- neither do I take- I ask no quarter- neither do I take any quarter- I am forever the same yesterday, today and tomorrow- I say the law changeth not- it is today as it was in the beginning "thou shall not kill- thou shall not trespass upon another- thou shall not covet another's possessions- thou shall not steal- thou shall not hate- thou shall love thine neighbor as thine self"-

So let it be- for this do I raise Mine voice, this day be ye as ones blest to hear that which I say unto thee-

For I am the Lord thy God

Sananda

Recorded by Thedra

FELLOWSHIP

Be Ye One

Mine children- This day I would speak unto thee of fellowship-

Fellowship is that which is given unto each of the brothers which know themself to be one- of one parent born: it is the common bond which bindeth them together as brothers- the communion and brotherhood of man under the Fatherhood of God our Eternal parent- wast it not said that all his sons shall be as one brother, as one child- and no separation - for it is clearly written that "there is no separation except in thine thinking"- ye shall be as one, not separate, one from the other- see that which is given unto Me to see the one flame which permeates thine forms- yet it is multiple in its action and it is great in its power- yet, thou hast not known such power as the three fold flame which permeates thine form- I say unto thee this is the power of God sent forth that ye might have thine being as man- such is Mine word unto thee this day- be ye as one- not divided-

So be it I Am the Lord thy God

Sananda

Responsibility

Be ye as Mine hand and say unto them in Mine name; that I, the Lord thy God hast spoken this day- and decreed for them their freedom- yet it is theirs to choose or reject- I say it is given unto them to be creatures of free will- and no man shall be unto them an ass- for they come of their own free will- they do not ride upon Mine back- I come that they might have freedom- yet I but point the way- I bring them not against their will- I say no man shall atone for them- they atone for their own willful way- their misused energy- there is no other way save by Me- I am the door- I am the one sent that they find their way- they come not save by Me- for I am the door, I am the <u>way</u>, the truth and the light- I am the door keeper- I guard well the door- I am not asleep! I say unto thee I am alert and I know Mine own- I give unto them passport- none other pass within the portals of Mine abode-

Be ye as ones prepared and be glad this day is come- let not thine foot slip- for I say unto thee there are many pitfalls- BE YE ALERT!

I am with thee that ye might have light so let it be--

I Am Sananda

Son of God the Father

Solen Aum Solen

Recorded by Thedra

Seek Thine Inheritance

Be ye as Mine hand made manifest unto them and say unto them as I would say- that the time is come when great light shall flood the Earth and great shall be the power thereof, for it is given unto Me the Lord thy God to be the one sent to prepare them to receive of it- I say "it is now come when great light shall flood the Earth, and great shall be the power thereof"

Now ye shall speak out-for the time is come when ye shall go forth and declare unto them the truth that He is come, the Lord of Hosts. I say unto them prepare ye the way for He is come, He is come- I bid them enter into the kingdom of the most high living God- I say: Arise, come ye out of the darkness and enter into the place of Mine abode and I shall give unto thee that which hast been kept for thee, for I am the one sent that ye might receive thine inheritance in full- let it be so-

The Father hast willed that ye have light, that ye return unto thine rightful estate- yet I tell thee of a surety thine fortune is not spent- it is kept for thee for this day- it is thine for the acceptance- thou hast been as ones blinded by the opinions and the will of men- yet I say unto thee ask of no man his opinion of or about Me for they too walk blindly-

I say ye, oh ye men of Earth, thou hast groped long in darkness and thine bondage hast been pitiful indeed- it is now come when I the Lord thy God bid thee arise- shake off thine leg irons and be ye as free men- sing ye a glad song! praise ye the name of our Father Eternal- be ye blest- for this do I come into the world of flesh- yet I tell thee; first, ye seek Me out then I shall reveal Mine self unto thee: fashion for thine self no idols- no images of Me for I am not of the Earth- I am of Mine Father sent that ye be free- seek Me in truth and in spirit and I shall reveal Mineself unto thee- be ye blest and rest in the knowing that I am come-

Flesh bindeth Me not- Earth binds Me not- thine laws bind Me not- for I am not of the Earth- I am free from <u>all</u> bonds- yet I say unto thee I am come that ye be free even as I- I Am that I Am-

Bless thine self for thine inheritance is a great and glorious one indeed- accept it, for this have I spoken unto thee thusly-

I am the Lord God

Sent of Mine Father

Solen Aum Solen-

The Father Eternal

Recorded by Thedra

They Shall Find No Hiding Place

Mine children- I say unto thee this day it is not a far off when every knee shall bend and every tongue shall ask of the Father forgiveness for their wonton and their waywardness- for I say unto thee they shall come to know the power which shall be unto them made manifest- I say they shall come to know that the Father is greater than all else- that He is and for this they have their being- for none shall deny Him: none shall be unto Him a stumbling block- yet I say unto them He is the all wise- all powerful Father, cause of thine being- yet they heed not that which I say- for they know Me not- now it is come when they shall be caught up short of their course and they shall stand in awe- they shall cry for mercy and forgiveness- they run hither and yon seeking a hiding place- but I have said unto them they shall find no hiding place- for there is none- no place is there wherein they might hide- I know wherein they are- I know Mine own too- and I shall find them and bring them out- now I say unto thee thou art of the chosen-- and thou art the chosen and for this do I say unto thee: enter into Mine place of abode as ones prepared- and be ye forever blest- let it be so- hasten ye to give unto them this word- and be ye as Mine hand made manifest unto them- I am with thee for I am not afar off- I Am

    Sananda

Hear Ye What the Spirit Sayeth

Sori Sori, be ye as the hand and foot of Me, the Lord thy God- fashion no false Gods for thine self - be ye true unto thine self and give unto the Father all the praise and the glory- hear ye what the spirit sayeth- give unto no man credit for thine salvation- be ye as ones responsible for thine own misused energy- and atone for all thine wanton ways- turn from them- repeat them <u>no more</u>- serve the Lord thy God with thine whole heart- and ask of <u>no man</u> his opinion- bless thine self by keeping thine own counsel- hear ye that which I say unto thee! be ye aware for many lie in wait to trip thee up- hasten ye to give unto them the word of God the Father- yet I say unto thee, <u>they</u> shall be responsible for that which they do with it. Ye shall not be held responsible for that which they do- for each shall be held accountable for his own deeds. Be ye as ones responsible for thine own- yet ye shall <u>not</u> give unto thine brother a stone when he asks for bread- I say unto thee be ye as ones prepared to feed Mine sheep- for I have given unto thee in great measure and Mine wares are not exhausted, I have plenty and to spare- I say unto thee they shall be given as they are prepared to receive- so let it be- thou art now prepared for thine new part-

    Praise ye the name of Solen Aum Solen-

Let thine joy fill thine cup to the brim, let them drink of the overflow- and be satisfied-

Such is Mine word unto thee this day- I am the Lord thy God-

Sananda

Recorded by Thedra

Behold

Behold! The day of the Lord is come! I say unto thee Behold! see that which I shall do; for I shall do a mighty work- I shall bring forth the mighty host to assist Mine chosen, I shall bring them out from the places wherein they labor for a pittance, I shall give unto them that which they have not known- I shall be unto them hand and foot- I shall put into their mouth words of wisdom- I shall place within their hand the sword of truth and justice, I shall place within their hands the reins of peace- I shall fill their hearts with peace- for I am <u>Justice</u>, I am <u>Peace</u>- I shall be unto them all the Father would have Me be- I say unto thee these things I shall do, and more- I say unto <u>them</u> which sleepeth: <u>AWAKEN</u> ye from thine sleep- come ye forth and walk which way I point! follow ye Me and be ye as ones prepared for I the Lord thy God hast spoken that ye might awaken- go ye forth and declare the "WORD" He the Lord thy God hast made known the laws, "follow ye Him" Be ye blest in the doing-

I say unto thee be ye swift to declare the word of the Lord for this have I given it unto thee-

Be ye blest this day and hasten ye that peace be established within thine own hearts--

This is Mine word unto thee this day-

I Am Sananda

I Am the I Am

Praise ye the name of Solen Aum Solen- hear that which He says unto thee- and be ye blest- I am the one sent that ye might hear- I am He which has power over the elements- I am the one which has power over the winds, the waters of the seas, the Earth, the fire, and I say unto thee- I AM the I AM- I AM that I AM- I Am not limited - neither am I bound of flesh-

I say unto thee thou art the mighty Sons of Israel- be ye as ones sent that there be light for thou art of Mine flock- Mine spirit-Mine chosen- I say unto thee Arise! Oh, ye mighty sons of Israel- for thou art of the House of Israel and thou art Divine in thine origin- be ye as ones free from all bondage and <u>arise</u> and return unto thine rightful estate- and ye shall be received as sons of God the Father, long away and there shall be great joy thruout the cosmos- let thine hearts rejoice this day is come when ye shall receive thine inheritance in full.

I AM that I AM

Sori Sori

Recorded by Thedra

The Asylum of The Solar System, S. K.

Most holy art thou oh, sons of God, be ye as ones blest, for it is Mine privilege to speak unto thee from out the inner temple wherein there is no darkness- I say unto thee- "wherein there is no darkness" So be it the darkness shall pass away and the light shall remain.

Now it is come when great shall be thine illumination and great thine service- so be it many shall come unto thee and they shall ask concerning the greater things and they too shall be as ones prepared for certain parts- for certain work- and they shall go forth as ones prepared for such as they shall be given to do-

There are many of the illumined ones which stand by to give unto thee assistance- and they ask nought of thee, <u>only</u> obedience unto the law- the service rendered, the plan fulfilled is their reward- the children of Earth little know of such devotion and service as these selfless ones know- fortune thine self the greater reward and be ye as ones forever blest-.

Bless thineself by thine selfless service- while it is given unto Me to serve the planetary system for long, I ask nothing more than its deliverance from bondage- the Earth is Mine part which concerns us most- for I say unto thee she the Earth hast been a wayward child- the asylum of the system and now it is come when she shall be cleansed and purified and brought forth as a shining orb- justified in her suffering, and all shall be made new- and great joy shall prevail- for this do we work without ceasing- let it be so with thee- let thine service be thine reward-

I bless thee this day--

I Am Sanat Kumara

Hold High Thine Own Banner

Beloved of Mine being- the time is come when the fields shall not yield up the supply sufficient to sustain the people and they shall cry out for food- they shall leave their battlefields that they might find food to sustain their bodies- many shall perish for lack of physical food-

Yet the ones which sit in high places shall declare war and sit in council for peace and they shall be as one which have the cross bones and the skeleton for their symbol- this is the banner which they serve under- while I say unto thee, ye shall carry high the banner of the cross and the crown- and ye shall know no want for I say unto thee ye shall be productive- and ye shall grow and be as ones blest- waste not thine time on the wanton ones- grieve not for them- hold high thine own banner and walk ye as "Sons of God"- arise this day and come ye into the fullness of thine estate for ye have but to claim it in the name of the Father Mother God- so shall it be a goodly fortune indeed- be ye as ones blest and I shall speak unto thee again and again for I have but begun-

I Am thine older Brother

Sanat Kumara

Recorded by Sister Thedra

To the Ones to Come

Beloved of Mine being- this day I would give unto thee of Mine strength, of Mine love- that ye might endure- yet ye shall draw forth from the source of thine being the substance which shall sustain thee- now I speak unto them which are come unto this altar- the time is come when each and every one shall come to know that this "Is the day of the Lord" and that He is come- while I say unto thee He is come- I too say they shall come unto Him in the time which is allotted unto them- for has He not gone before thee to prepare a place- now let it be understood that the day of preparation shall pass and they which are unprepared shall be found wanting- for none enter into His place of abode unprepared- let this be remembered- while it is yet time I speak unto the ones which shall come- they shall come in holy remembrance- and for the communication with Him which is the Lord thy God- they shall be as sibets- as candidates for the greater revelation- then they shall have the assistance and guidance necessary unto their initiation- forget not this is the path of initiation- and let it be remembered that there are none so sad as the ones which betray themself-

I say unto thee they are the saddest of the lot- while I am the one known as the worthy Grand Master- I say it is Mine duty to speak unto them of certain things which concerns them- first, <u>Love ye one</u> another- serve selflessly- and with joy- hear ye the words which is given unto them and be ye as ones prepared to give of thine self without reservation- unto them which have not the "word" neither the strength nor the desire to learn- yet ye shall be as ones blest to offer up thine self on their behalf- ye shall not in <u>any way</u> trespass upon their free will- neither shall ye bring them against their will- I say unto thee be ye as the candidate for the greater learning-

While much hast been given unto thee- there is yet more- close not thine ears- (or) thine hand- reach out that it might serve the greater plan- for this have I spoken that ye might be part of the greater and divine plan- let it be so--

I Am thine older brother and Sibor known as

The Most Worthy Grand Master

Recorded by Thedra

Sananda Speaks unto the Father

Most holy Father Mother God. I give unto thee all the praise- all the glory- I bring unto thee these thine children which have asked of Me, that they be delivered up into thine keeping I give them- for this Mine part I am finished- I have come into their midst that they might come to know thee. O, Father I come unto them as thou hast sent Me, of Mine own free will I come- now I give of Mineself that they might come to know the joy which is given unto one which hast returned unto thee-

Be it so Father that they all return unto thee with Me, for this is the time of fulfillment for these thine children- for this have I revealed Mineself unto them-

Now I say unto them: <u>hear ye that which I say unto Mine Father for He and I are one. I know Mineself to be one with Him</u>--

Glad am I that I am privileged to come unto them Father that they might be prepared to return unto thee with Me- I Am Glad! So be it

Father that this is My part and I have accepted it in thine name and unto thine glory shall it be finished-

Be it so that they shall follow in Mine footsteps and go with Me where I go- let it be as thou hast willed it-

I Am Thine Son

Sananda

This Day Shall Bear Fruit

Behold the hand of God made manifest- see that which He shall do- see the manifestations of the word, for I say unto thee the word hast gone out from His mouth that this day shall bear fruit; new fruit such as thou hast not tasted of- let it be the fulfillment of all thine labors- for I say all thine labors shall be as one account- they shall be added up- and they shall be weighed in the balance and there shall be no lack- for I have said it shall be fulfilled- the end shall be a glorious triumph and ye shall stand as the victor- and triumphant shall ye return unto thine abiding place- I say ye shall return unto thine abiding place victorious and thine joy shall know no bounds- so shall it be a glad day-

I Am with thee this day

I Am Sananda

Recorded by Thedra

Love

This day I would speak unto thee of love- it is now come when ye shall come to know the meaning of "LOVE", for it thou art sustained- I say unto thee because of the love which we bear for thee art thou sustained- while We thine benefactors work without ceasing that the great and divine plan be brought to fulfillment. Thou dost weary of body- yet ye shall remember that thine body is but a fragment of thine own creation which shall change and change as the rainbow colors- While I say unto thee O, Mine beloved ones thou art not mortal flesh- thou art of light substance which shall not pass away- which shall not perish- neither is it bound by flesh- listen ye unto Mine words; for I say unto thee: "<u>thou art not mortal flesh</u>" thou art a threefold being- and ye shall not die- for thou art eternal beings- thou art beings of light substance which perish not- be ye as ones which <u>know</u>- know ye that I dwell with thee- that I am the Lord thy God- and I shall bless thee this day- ask of no man his opinion for I say unto thee man's opinions are such that they trip thee up- let thine feet be planted firmly upon the rock which I Am- for I Am the Son of God - sent that ye might return unto Him the Father with Me-

I AM

Sananda

The Father Speaks

Beloved of Mine being I speak unto thee out the fullness of Mine being- and words can not express the fullness of Mine love- Mine being- for thee- for I say unto thee thou art of Me and by Me- for I am thine Father which hast brought thee forth from the beginning of thine existence as a personality- I say unto thee thou art Mine creation - for from Mine being hast thou come forth- let thine hands be Mine, thine mind be Mine- for I say unto thee thou art of Me and without thee I should not be whole- for without thee I should not be perfect-

I am no less for sending thee forth- I am no more for bringing thee home- yet Mine joy shall be great when ye return unto Me- there is great joy in the cosmos when a Son returns unto his abiding place and receives his inheritance- ye shall come to know for I say it is now come when thine bondage shall end- and ye shall return unto Me unscathed, unharmed- for this have I sent Mine Sons that ye might awaken unto thine identity- I say unto thee remember thine inheritance is greater than all the wealth of the Earth- yea that of the Solar System- for all I have is thine- be ye as Sons of God thine Father- walk ye as such amongst thine fellow men and be ye as ones prepared to return unto Me- so be it there shall be great joy throughout the cosmos- so shall it be- as I have sent forth a fiat that it be so- so let it be-

I Am thine Father

Solen Aum Solen

Recorded by Thedra

Ye Shall Be Unveiled

Mine children rest in the knowing that thou art the Sons of God the Father- born of Him art thou- brought forth through His mercy by His

grace- and because of His love shall ye be brought back unto thine abiding place-

Now it is written that ye shall come to know Him the Father as I know Him, yet it is given unto thee to be sorely oppressed- yet I tell thee thine oppression shall be as nought- for it shall pass and ye shall stand forth as the sentinels of light- the Sons of God which thou art- I say ye shall be unveiled and ye shall step forth as the Sons of God which thou art- let not the veil blind thee for I tell thee it is but the flesh which blinds thee- it is the veil of illusion, be ye not deceived- while I say unto thee the illusion shall pass and ye shall stand as the sentinels of light which thou art- thou hast been brought forth as such- while thou hast seen the flesh and called it "self" I tell thee it is the illusion- for the reality is that which is and shall ever be without end-

So be it the <u>endless</u>- for there is nothing which is <u>real</u> which shall pass- that which is endless changes as the Sun, as the colors of the rainbow scintillate- as the colors of the borealis- and takes unto itself greater and grander forms- while the Sun is the Sun it never is less for its many rays which go out from it- hear ye that which I say unto thee and be ye of a mind to learn- for the forms of man changeth and changeth from one into another, and ever greater more perfect shall they become until thine eyes could not behold such perfection as that of the glorified man- I say unto thee: thine eyes could not look upon such perfection as the "glorified man"- so be it that thine eyes shall be made to see- for thine eyes shall be opened and thine mind quickened and ye shall behold Him in all His glory- So be it and Selah-

I have spoken and thou hast heard Me-

I Am Sananda

The Love We Bear

This day be ye reminded of the love which we bear for thee- for I say unto thee it is because and for that love which we bear that We stand by to give unto thee assistance, I tell thee of such love yet thou can not comprehend the fullness of such while thou art looking amongst men- for no man knoweth such love of himself-

Yet such love *is* and shall ever be: for this do I say unto thee let thine service be selfless- selfless love brings selfless service- and selfless service the greater reward - the GREATER REWARD is thine INHERITANCE--

Such is Mine word unto thee this day- so be it I am the Lord thy God-

Sananda

Recorded by Thedra

The Father Speaks: Of His Son

Beloved children- the time is come when I have sent Mine Sons unto thee in great numbers, that ye be brought out of darkness- released from thine bondage- yet I say unto thee- thou hast not shaken off thine leg iron- thine opinions, thine preconceived ideas of Me thine Father which hast sent these Mine Sons to awaken thee-

Now I say unto thee: these are Mine children- these are Mine Sons and Mine Daughters which I have sent forth that this Mine word might

be made known to thee- I say unto thee these which I have sent into the world of man are Mine hands, Mine feet made manifest unto thee that ye might come to know thine origin, thine own identity- I say unto thee thou hast lost thine way- "The Word" hast been sealed up against the rebellious ones that it might not be pilfered and misused-

While I say unto thee, hear that which I say and keep "The Word" sacred and holy- be ye not so foolish as to adulterate it for it is but the greater part of foolishness- I say unto thee I am and I am thine Father eternal- I have brought thee forth: from out Mine mouth did I speak the word which hast given unto thee being.

Now ye shall be as ones prepared for thine return- I send Mine Son which I have chosen unto them which are prepared to receive Him- that He might touch them and be made whole- I tell thee- ye shall be as one prepared, for He shall find thee by thine own light in the place wherein ye are- ye shall walk upright, honorable in His sight- forget not He sees thee for that which thou art- give not the bitter cup unto any man- hear ye that which he has to say unto thee for I have sent Him unto thee as Mine own Son, appointed by and of Me for this His part- this part is not new unto Him for He hast come many times as Mine hand made manifest unto thee- He is Mine hand, Mine foot, Mine voice- Hear ye Him and follow ye Him- for I say unto thee He is come that ye might be prepared to return unto Me with Him--

I say unto thee He Mine Son is the one which I have chosen from among the host which is come unto thee- that ye might awaken and return unto Me with Him; for He is the Lord of Lords, the Lord of Hosts- ye shall be as one blest to receive Him- I speak out this day that ye might come into the fullness of thine being- I am not finished,

I AM the Father- I AM the Mother- I AM the Son.

Solen Aum Solen

Recorded by Thedra

Christmas -

Blest are they which remember Me sayeth the Lord thy God, blest are they which keep the law-- blest are they which go with Me for I am come that they which are prepared might return unto Mine Father with Me--.

This is the day of remembrance when they come to know that which hast been hidden from them- I say unto them which seek light- this is the age of light- the time of knowing- and all which are prepared shall come into the fullness of their being- for it is written that this is the time of the end and the time of the new beginning- the old shall pass away and the new shall be established so let it be as the Father hast willed it.

This is the day of putting off the old- taking up the new- and the old shall pass away as nothing, and be no more- the new order shall be established and all which are prepared shall dwell in the house of the Lord--.

I say unto these which are prepared- come ye out from among the hypocrites and the transgressors and let thine light shine that they might see it- be ye no part of their hypocrisy, their blasphemy-- ask of them nought except obedience unto the law- waste not thine time on them--

for I say unto thee it is thine part to obey the law and let thine own light shine that they might see it and be drawn unto it*--.

Blest are they which seek truth and justice for they shall be justified by the law- wast it not said that justice shall prevail- for it is the will of Mine Father which hast sent Me.

So be it I Am

Sananda

*Teach by example

Recorded by Sister Thedra

The Lord's Compassion

Sanat Kumara speaking- Beloved of Mine being- it is with great compassion that we wait for them which are yet in bondage- yet they shall be as ones bound until they choose to come of their own will- I would say unto them: there are great and powerful ones which await to give thee assistance, when ye choose to accept it- they which are of a mind to accept such assistance shall be glad indeed.

For this do We the Sibors wait with longing in our heart, for we know such freedom as thou hast not remembered- while it is the law that ye be of a mind to receive and to accept that which We bring- I say, there is none so pitiful as the ones which reject us, that which We have for them- the Sibors draweth nigh unto the Earth that She might be lifted up- while it is the place of the laggards- there are many which have gone out from their abiding* place that they might be found and brought home- I say- some have foresworn their own freedom that others might be freed from bondage. While they have wandered under the cover of night**- others have followed after them that they might be awakened unto their divinity and brought back--.

I tell thee, they are divine in their origin, in their progression and therein is a great story***- the drama of the Earth and the Heavens are written therein--

I say unto thee: be ye as ones playing the greatest drama of all times. Know thine self to be participants within this great play and be ye as ones remembering that which ye do and have done--

Seek ye the light- ask and ye shall receive--

Be ye blest for the seeking- rest in the knowing the Lord thy God is come-

So be it I shall speak again and again--

I AM Sanat Kumara

Recorded by Thedra

*Origin/home

** darkness/unknowing- they too fell asleep-

*** The Prodigal Son

New Year! New Day!

Beloved ones- this day I would say unto thee the time is come for the sifting and the sorting- (the harvest) and this is the day for which ye have waited- the day of the end- <u>the end time</u>, when thine wandering shall be finished, completed, finished to be repeated no more--

Now while it is so- I tell thee ye shall prepare thine self for a new beginning- thine new part- what a glorious new part is prepared for thee, and what a glorious new day thou art beginning and what a bountiful harvest it shall be- let it be a time of rejoicing! Look unto the mountain from whence cometh great strength and see the glory of that which lies before thee: let thine hearts rejoice for this day- be ye glad it is come- look unto the East see the sun cometh up from out the East- know ye that there is a plan far greater than man hast imaged-be ye as one and sing within thine heart songs of gladness- so let it go out unto all which are prepared to receive the new day for great shall be the light which shall flood the Earth and all which receive of it shall be made to rejoice. Let it be so with thee-.

Be ye at Peace and poise---

I AM the Lord thy God

Sananda

Ones to Come

Blessed are they which come unto this altar for they shall be given comprehension- I say: "they shall be given comprehension" let it be so-for this do I bring them- I say unto thee for <u>this</u> do I bring them that they might be given comprehension-

Now there are ones which shall come which have little comprehension, and <u>these</u> shall be as ones prepared for the next part which shall be given unto them- I say unto thee give them nought which would choke them- for they would but <u>choke</u>- the way is open, and the time is come when ye shall receive them and prepare them for the next step- yet some shall <u>not</u> step forth as ones able to walk forth under their own strength or by their own efforts: let not these ride thine back- for I say unto thee they shall put forth the effort and they shall be rewarded So be it I have spoken and thou hast heard Me-

I Am Sananda

Recorded by Thedra

Peace

Beloved Ones - the time is come when I shall prove mineself - and they shall come to know that I AM, the Lord thy God. I have spoken and mine words shall not return unto me void for I say unto thee - the word hast power they know not of-

While it is given unto them to go into battle one with the other, I the Lord thy God see the end - the end of all their wonton -- their willfulness - their aggression-

I say it is come when they shall sit at the counsel table and ask for peace - Yet they shall find no peace - for peace is not within them -- I

say unto them look within for peace - let it be within thine own heart - wait not upon another to establish peace for thee - "Be ye at Peace" and peace shall reign amongst them---for first it must be established within the heart - While I say unto each of them Peace, Peace, Peace, they clamor for war - they betray themself for this is the great pity---they have not had the Peace which I know---While I AM come that Peace be established - I do not find Peace amongst them---neither within them. Let it be established now that I AM come that they might find Peace--Yet it shall first be within their heart----

For this have I spoken---

So let it be that mine word shall be established within thine heart this day. Each one hast been blest to be within the sound of mine voice so be it - I AM Sananda

Son of God -

Silence

BELOVED OF MINE BEING: THIS DAY I would say unto thee: be ye alert and fortune thineself the part of wisdom, for I say unto thee the silence which is necessary unto thine learning is of great importance-- no word can convey unto thee that which can be imparted unto thee through silence---I say silence is of great importance unto us- for in the silence can we reach thee---be ye as ones prepared and for this do I speak of silence.

While it is given unto thee to communicate through the spoken word- it is given unto thee to hear that which we say unto thee with thine inner ear- So be it that we speak unto thee in words which are not heard by the outer ear. It is of a different frequency - and not audible unto thee when thou art speaking---silence is the key which hast to be turned for us to enter in through thine door.

Be ye blest this day---

I AM Thine Brother and thine Sibor Bor -

Recorded by Sister Thedra

Solen Aum Solen

Blest are Mine hands and Mine feet- for they shall be Mine servants- they shall be unto Me all that I would have them be- for I shall put forth the energy and the will which shall be sufficient unto them- they shall not falter neither shall they wither away- nor be severed from Me- for they are members of Mine body and these are of Mine being and I am not of a mind to sacrifice them- be ye as Mine hand and Mine feet for I have expanded Mine being- Mineself, and I have called thee Mine children- while thou hast forgotten thine source, I say unto thee: I am the source of being, I have sent thee forth as Mine foot and as Mine own I have put thee upon Mine beloved orb which I have used for a footstool- and I have written thine name in the book of life- I have given unto thee a number, a color and a time- A place I have provided thee--

I say unto thee thou art not alone, for I have provided for thee- for I am not a forgetful Father- I am mindful of thee- for thou hast given unto Me cause to remember thee- I have given unto thee cause to remember Me- for thou art <u>not</u> separate from Me- <u>NOW</u>, I have given forth a mandate that ye shall be found and brought back- that ye be given that which hast been kept for thee, and it is indeed a princely fortune- glad ye shall be when ye come to know that which hast been hidden from thee--.

Be ye as the hand and foot and I shall quicken thee and ye shall see and know thine divinity- thine oneness with Me-

I say, arise, and rejoice for I have spoken out and thou hast heard Me-

Let it ever be so--

I Am thine Father

Solen Aum Solen

Recorded by Thedra

Oh Father: - Sananda

Almighty Father, Father, oh Father hast thine children not forgotten the glory which wast theirs! Oh, Father I go unto them as thine hand made manifest- I speak unto them that which thou givest unto Me for them-

Now Father I ask for them that they might become aware of their own divinity and awaken unto the fullness of their inheritance, bring them out of bondage oh Father, for thine love encompasses all of thine own creation- for this do I say unto them thine love is sufficient unto all thine creation- and wast it not so they should perish from the Earth- I speak unto thee Father as thine son which knowest the fullness of thine love- I would that they knew as I do- be it as thou hast willed it, for this have I offered up Mineself as a living sacrifice- Father I thank thee for the privilege of giving of Mineself that they might come to know thee as I do-

While they are as yet bound in darkness- let them be comforted by the word and it shall be sufficient unto them: for hast it not been said that I shall give unto them that which they need, and is it not so--- Be they blest of Me as thou hast blest Me Father-

So Might it Be-

Be it so that

I Am thine Son

Sent that they be blest--

I Am

Sananda

Recorded by Thedra

Thou Dost Make Thine Own Environment

Be ye as Mine hand made manifest unto them- and say unto them as I would there is a time and a place allotted unto them- there is a place prepared for them and each shall be placed in his rightful place, for it is known unto us which stand by to assist-

I tell thee none are put into the place wherein they are not fit- the place for each one is a suitable one- and none shall be out of his own proper place- each one shall be accounted for and by his own light and vibration shall he be known--

He can find no place to hide--

For there is NO hiding place- for each one is known and his whereabouts is no secret- that which he does is known and it shall be revealed openly-

While I say unto them they shall be found and put into their proper place- it is now the time to alert thineself and prepare a place of greater grandeur for thine self- for there shall be many steps before thee; many paths- many mansions, many resting places- it is said that ye shall be put into thine own environment- make of it what ye will- for as ye will it so shall it be- for I say unto thee-

And each unto his own- let it suffice that thou hast free will and thou hast had the "WORD" and it shall be unto thee sufficient for it contains the law- and the "GOLDEN KEY". Be ye as ones prepared to enter into the Holy of Holies- for this hast the "KEY" been placed within thine hand. So be it that I am the keeper of the gate and none pass without the light which binds thee unto Me- the light I AM-

The Lord thy God hast spoken--

Be ye of a mind to hear that which I say-

I AM Sananda

Recorded by Thedra

Mighty and Strong is the Hand of God

Sori Sori- Mighty is the hand of God - it is with power that it is wielded and it is with wisdom- herein I would say unto thee- be ye as ones prepared for the day of the Lord is at hand- I say that Mighty and Strong is the hand of God- it shall sweep clean all the filth, all the unclean which is created by man- and there shall be no place left for them which are want to destroy His handiwork- ye shall see the hand of God move- it shall move upon the land, upon the waters and it shall be given unto them which are want to destroy the works of God to perish from the face of the Earth- and they shall be no more loosened upon the Earth for they shall be bound-- and they shall learn that there is no power on Earth which can equal that of God the Father's for He is the might and strong; above all others for He is the Father-

Let it be said herein that he is that which was before them and shall ever be- worlds without end He hast created- and He hast peopled them and brought forth that which He hast called His Sons- and He hast given them dominion over the planets which He hast created and He hast set the planets into motion and put His Sons over them- He hast begotten Angels for to care for the lesser creations that they too might fulfill their destiny and He hast not forgotten His own--

Yet I say unto thee ye shall remember Him and be ye blest in the doing- give unto Him thanks and praise and all the glory- for this have I spoken unto thee-

Give unto them which are come to destroy no credit- no credence, for they shall be disarmed-

I say unto thee <u>SEE</u> the hand of God move- and be ye glad--.

So Be it

I AM Sananda

Recorded by Thedra

I Am That I Am

Sori Sori- Blest art thou this day, blest shall ye be, for I am the Lord thy God, come that ye be blest, So shall it be- for the time is come when ye shall go forth as ones which have the power and the authority to call thineself Sons of God-

Ye shall walk in Mine footsteps, ye shall go where I go- ye shall know as I know- ye shall do Mine work- ye shall be unto them Sibor even as I am unto thee; for this have I sibored thee- I say unto thee: "for this have I sibored thee"-- Be ye as ones illumined even as I- for I say unto thee I am come that it be so- so let it be as the Father hast willed it- I speak unto thee from out the fullness of Mine being, for I am that I Am- I am not limited! I say unto thee <u>thou art holy</u> Mine beloved ones, holy in thine origin- be ye aware of thine divinity- for is it not given unto thee to be of "Divine Origin"? Discount not thine self.

For I say unto thee thou art the holy ones of Isreal- come into the Earth that there be light- so be ye aware of thine part- carry Mine lamp high, cast no shadows before it-

Now ye shall be as ones blameless for these Mine words, no man shall treat them lightly- for I say unto thee O, blessed ones, I am responsible for that which I do, that which I say unto thee, now ye shall give unto them these Mine words that they might know that which I say unto thee- that they might bear witness of Mine words- so let it be for their own enlightenment- I Am that I Am-

Sananda, Son of the Most High Living God-

Solen Aum Solen

For Those Who See the Lord

Beloved ones- there are great and mighty ones which stand guard for the ones which have the strength of character to follow in Mine footsteps- I say unto thee there is a mighty host which stands ready to assist them which have a mind to follow in Mine footsteps- while I say unto them: "follow ye Me" many have not the strength of character to follow Me- I say unto thee I am the Lord thy God- sent that the way be made clear before them- yet I say they stand as ones deaf- as ones with feet of lead- they move not for they are given unto false doctrines and preconceived ideas of and about Me-

Now it is come when many shall inquire of Me- and ye shall give unto them this word: They shall be as ones prepared to enter into the holy of holies for none other shall enter- they shall have no preconceived ideas of or about Me- they shall come empty- the heart shall be filled to overflowing with love for all men- they shall be of a mind to go where I lead them, they shall be humble of heart- they shall be as ones blest- they shall have peace within them- they shall have no malice within them- they shall be as the initiate- they shall walk gently before their fellow men- they shall not be given unto slander, nor flattery- they shall give no offence- neither shall they take offence of their brothers- they shall be as brothers- they shall go the last mile with him gladly- with joy in their heart- such is Mine word unto them which shall inquire of thee, that which I have said unto thee shall suffice them which seek Me- So let it be I am the Lord thy God-

Sananda

Oh, Mighty Sons of God

Mother eternal am I- I bid thee come unto Me, thine Mother eternal and be ye forever blest- I say unto thee thou art Mine children: children of Mine bosom, brot forth from out the being of the first cause, the first and last, the Alpha the Omega- I say unto thee thou art holy beings: beings eternal art thou, while it is so thou hast wandered in bondage lo the eons of time, I say it is now come when ye shall come into the fullness of thine estate for have I not remembered thee in thine wanderings? Have I not known thee and kept thee, Oh ye eternal children of Mine own heart- I await thine return- filled with longing hast thou been: while thou hast not remembered thine days with Me, I say unto thee thou shall remember as thou hast been filled with longing, so hast thou heart been filled with sorrow- yet Mine beloved children thine longing shall be satisfied and thine sorrow shall be no more-

I say unto thee Mine blessed children thou shall return unto Me unscathed- untouched- unchanged- for I am thine Mother, boundless is Mine love for thee- be ye blest this day- and be ye as Mine hand, as Mine mouth, Mine feet, be ye swift to do the work which is given unto thee- swift to do the work of the Lord thy God- Joyful that this day is come- walk ye in the light- sing ye praise unto the Father, be ye as sons which hast returned- Joyful shall be the peons of praise and glad shall be the hearts of them which return unto Me this day- I say unto thee- Hail, Hail unto thee Oh Mighty Sons of God it is now come when thy return is assured- so be it thru His mercy and grace-

I Am thine Mother Sarah

Recorded by Thedra

Pure Spirit Is Fresh

Mine children- children of Mine bosom art thou: from Mine own bosom hast thou been nurtured- from Mine own bosom hast thou been sustained--

For this hast thou been maintained the physical body, for this hast thou the power, the strength to keep thine feet upon the ground - thine eyes open- thine mouth to speak- thine hands to move- I say unto thee I am thine eternal Mother- and I am that which hast kept thee from destruction- I have protected, nourished and maintained thine physical body- thine spirit is eternal and passeth not away- while I say unto thee matter is within a constant change- spirit takes upon itself that which is of matter for that which serves its purpose- yet "Spirit" is not limited by the pore, by matter- it moves as "Spirit"- it permeates; it moves,- as it goes and comes freely it passes and stagnates not- I say unto thee pure spirit is <u>fresh,</u> it is like unto a fresh downpour of summer rain- it is fresh it is not stagnant! it is that which refreshes and vivifies! I say unto thee be ye as ones refreshed by the spirit- for that I am-

I Am thine Mother Eternal- I Am thine Mother Sarah from whence thou hast come into manifestation- So be it I Am the spirit of the holy breath.

The Most Sacred Word

Mine beloved children there is a mighty power within the word of Solen Aum Solen- I have said unto thee there is great power in the word Solen Aum Solen- It is the word which shall be most sacred unto thee- it is the one word which shall be unto thee thine shield and thine buckler- it is the name of the Father which hast kept thee for this day-

Mine beloved ones this name, Solen Aum Solen is sacred above all others- hold it ever within thine heart- speak it with remembrance and reverence- for I say unto thee thou art mighty sons of the eternal Father Solen Aum Solen- He hast <u>for</u> <u>this</u> <u>day</u> released a new fiat that ye shall be brought out of bondage- this He has decreed! I tell thee of a truth- this He hast decreed that ye be brought out of bondage- I speak unto thee now that ye might know that which hast been sent forth as a mighty fiat; that ye might be as the sons which thou art-.

Know ye this: no man shall rob thee of thine inheritance- no man shall turn thee out. Forfeit not thine inheritance, be ye forever blest and be ye forever free- even as I am free- arise put on the whole armor of God- and bless thineself as ye would that I bless thee- ask of no man his blessings- for I say unto thee bless thine self- I have blessed thee with <u>Mine</u> <u>love</u>, <u>Mine</u> <u>life</u>, Mine energy-

I shall not forsake thee for I am the Lord thy God Sananda

Recorded by Thedra

Ye Shall Choose

Behold! This is a new day! and I say unto thee this is the day in which ye shall go forth rejoicing that it is come- I say: this day ye shall go forth with great joy within thine heart that <u>this</u> day is come, that the Lord thy God is with thee- that we have communion one with the other- that the time is come when ye shall be brought out of bondage- when ye are released from the wheel of rebirth- when ye shall fulfill thine own mission and return unto thine abiding place- I say unto thee: ye shall choose wherein ye shall serve- ye shall be as ones prepared to Sibor them which are yet in bondage, or ye might choose yet other realm beyond that which thou hast not known- so be it ye are free to choose where ye serve- yet serve the light ye shall- I say ye shall choose to serve the light from whence thou hast come- so be it as the Father hast willed it- I the Lord thy God sayeth unto thee- ye shall choose wherein ye shall serve- for serve ye shall- for art thou not of the ones sent that the world of man be lifted up-

I say unto thee thou hast volunteered to serve that <u>they</u> be lifted up- so be it that thou hast not remembered thine days of service with Me, ere this one- while I say unto thee thou hast chosen to follow Me- thou hast chosen the same path which I have gone- yet too I say unto thee there are differences of opinions about Me- and of Mine path- Mine part- yet it matters not what <u>they</u> say- what they <u>think</u>: I say unto <u>them</u> they know not that which I shall do- for I have not revealed Mine hand unto <u>them</u>- I have not given unto <u>them</u> the secrets which I hold- for this do I say unto <u>them</u> "prepare thine self to receive Me and of Me"- So be it they shall divest themself of their preconceived ideas of Me and about Me, so be it they shall have a mind to follow in Mine footsteps- go where I go.

I Am the Lord thy God- I have spoken and thou hast heard Me. Praise ye the Name of Solen Aum Solen- unto Him all the praise, all the glory! Forever and forever! So be it-

I Am Sananda

Behold

Beloved ones- while it is yet time I say unto thee there are many which are prepared to enter into the place of Mine abode, yet they know it not for as yet they have not awakened unto their divinity- while it is given unto Me to know them, they know not- Now it is given unto Me to say unto them <u>AWAKEN</u>! Awaken unto thine divinity! Oh, ye sons of God, the Father hast given unto thee everlasting life- and thou hast not known of thine inheritance- for that matter thou hast forgotten Him, the Source of thine being- let it be that ye shall remember Him and the estate which thou hast forfeited ere thou didst descend into bondage- Behold! Behold! I say unto thee Behold! See that which I shall do-

I am the Lord thy God

Sananda

Recorded by Thedra

Thou Knowest Unknowingly

Beloved children- I say unto thee this day- Mine hand is firm and strong- Mine mercy is great and far reaching- while thou knowest not the fullness of Mine mercy I say unto thee it is great indeed- and for this have I sent Mine sons unto the Earth that it might have light- that the ones in bondage might be delivered up- now I speak unto thee that ye might come to know thine part- that ye might know that thou art not forgotten- I say ye have wandered long, knowing not that ye know- while I say unto thee thou knowest unknowingly- now the time draweth nigh when the veil shall be rent and be as nothing and ye shall remember thine sonship- thine true identity and ye shall be glad- for I say unto thee Mine children thine inheritance is a princely one indeed and thou art sons of God- most holy, most divine is thine estate- I say unto thee be ye not deceived by appearance for it is of the world of man and shall pass as the illusion which it is- be ye as sons of the most high living God Solen Aum Solen- Which I AM.

Mine children there are ones who know not that I Am- while thou art aware of Mine existence, thou art not aware of the fullness of Mine being: for this do I say unto thee: be ye as one- as one not divided against thine self- for thou art one and thou art of one parent born- thou art whole within the One- while thou appear to be separate within the world of man- I say unto thee thou art not separate one from the other- for the Father hast brought forth the first born generation as one creation which was perfect in its completion- and then one which wast amongst them- that generation didst betray himself and create that which brought about the illusion which is not, nor never was, of our Father- for I say unto thee our Father creates perfect and complete- while thou hast seen that which is of the "world of illusion". Thou hast not seen with thine natural eyes the reality of the first born- Now hear ye that which I say unto thee: there are ones which walketh as man in appearance which are not of this order- these are the "sons of perdition", these are the soulless ones which are not of the first generation- which are the sons of God- the eternal beings which shall return unto him as they went out from Him pure in essence- justified in their Search for the ones which have wandered in bondage- I say unto thee thine wandering shall end and thine wanderings shall be justified- now I say be ye as <u>one</u>, let thine light so shine that they which are bound might see it and be drawn unto it as the moth unto the flame- I say unto thee- Hail! Hail unto thee- return unto thine abiding place and wander no more- for I have prepared the way before thee; so shall it be a great day- and I am glad-

I Am Sananda

Recorded by Thedra

Responsibilty for the Word

Beloved ones: Mighty is the power of the word and I say unto thee this day ye shall go forth as the voice of one come into thine midst- ye shall declare unto them that "This is the day of salvation" "This is the day of the Lord" and this is the truth for which they have waited- I speak now of the ones which yet have not stirred out of their tracks- I speak of the ones which think themself wise- I speak unto thee that they might come to know that which is in store for them- to awaken them unto their true identity- I speak unto thee that it be done for them- yet I tell thee it is not thine responsibility what they do with the word, when they have received it- for it then <u>becomes</u> <u>their</u> <u>own</u> responsibility- I tell thee of a surety thou shall not be held accountable for that which they do with "the word" when they have received it- yet I say unto thee: change not one word- for these are sacred unto Me- I waste not mine energy on frivolity- be ye ever mindful of this - for I am the Lord thy God- sent that there be light- bring them in and give of thineself that they might come to know the truth- be ye blest in the doing-

I say unto thee be ye blest in the doing- I Am that I Am

Sananda

Recorded by Thedra

It is well to call for peace but a great many of the lifestreams upon this this planet have no understanding of peace, indeed they were brought into embodiment at this critical time in the evolution of this planet for the express purpose of helping the lifestreams of Earth to pay up the heavy Karma they have made.

After the old is destroyed, all the set patterns of ancient evil are shaken up and scattered so that they can never again express in the old negative ways. Then the new shall be built in the great Golden age patterns and all who mourned the passing of the old, upon seeing the splendor of the new, will proclaim it "well done" and worth all the anguish. it is well known that before the new can be built the old must be removed. This causes much hardship at the time of removal but after the beautiful new construction begins to take form, all the old worthless forms are forgotten. That is the way it must be.

Brace yourself for the time of cleansing, keep your mind on the goal and it will not be so great a trial.

REMEMBER THE GOAL

I AM SANANDA KNOWN AS JESUS

Mind Stuff

Be ye as ONE with ME, for this have I come unto thee; that ye may know that which I have for thee and it is now come when I shall Sibor thee in the way of 'Mind' - have I not said I would say more on the subject - and is it not so? Let it be so.

I say unto thee MIND is that which is given unto thee of God the Father and it is thy inheritance from HIM - thy endowment - and fortuned unto thee by and of HIM.

Now let it be stated, that when they are feeble-minded, they are NOT SO by HIM, nor has HE willed it so! Neither has HE taken from them his gift of mind-stuff, they have fortuned such condition unto themself. And it is fortuned unto every man which cometh into the world to have free-will and when he uses it WELL, for the GLORY of GOD the Father, he is as one given greater mind capacity, greater gifts, and he has been as one given his inheritance in full; yet when one betrays himself and uses his gifts for his selfish end, and for the sense-gratification and to give unto his fellows the bitter cup, he is one which betrays his trust himself - his fellows, and turns his face from his SOURCE: and he forfeits his gifts for a time, until he learns his bitter lesson, and he then is reinstated into the House of the Father - with full-honors, as a SON and a full-inheritor of the kingdom of God and then may call himself a Son: and be it not robbery to call himself "God" for Truly, is it not so? For has he ever been LESS? For did the Father not make him so? And did he not forfeit his inheritance for self: Which he has fortuned unto SELF?

Yet let this be understood: that to become God, and to become One with God the Father is to Know THYSELF; which is God.

Now was it not said that in the beginning God created man in His image and is it not so? He, the Father, made Himself a living CREATURE and breathed upon it and it became a LIVING SOUL. So it is clearly written, that he BECAME a living SOUL and that "image" which the Father did fashion "IMAGE" became a living soul by the breath which the Father, did breathe forth into His image this LIVING CREATURE.

Now it is said this living creature did turn his face from the source of his being and he did forfeit his inheritance and some of his gifts were taken from him and he became self: the animal-self'; which is the chemical-man or the hu-MAN, and he is the animated creature mindless, shall we say? Void of this mind of GOD which was endowed unto him in the beginning -

Now we shall explain this further, at another - Let us say, this living creature goes into the world as a pore, (which we call "MAN") and he walks with God the Father, he serves Him as His Son, he remembers his source and he gives unto the Father credit for his BEING - he gives unto HIM, the Father, credit, glory and praise and he walks upright as "MAN" - He glorifies the Father as the Father has glorified him. And he is endowed with certain 'gifts' and he draws upon his inheritance as need be and he claims his right and his SONSHIP which is lawful, and there is no limitation of a Son of God - for I say unto thee - the Mind of God the Father is fathomless and perfect - it is the omnipresent and omnipotent. I say it is fathomless and omnipresent!

Now I shall speak at length on this subject at a later hour. Blessings be upon thee this day - I AM Berean.

By my hand shall ye be blest this day - for I come that ye be blest of me, thy older Brother. Be ye as one prepared to receive ME. I AM he which has come unto thee to give unto thee the discourse on "Mind" and I say unto thee it is my part and it is my joy, for I am as one prepared for this part. For it is for my preparation that I am able to Sibor thee in this manner, for I know the law governing such matters.

Now when ye become efficient in the law ye shall sibor others, even as we, thy Sibors, have sibored thee. I say WHEN ye become efficient in the law ye shall sibor others, even as we thy Sibors have sibored thee. Then, ye have earned the right to call thyself Sibor/Teacher/Master; and by any other name which indicates MASTERY. Yet ye shall not deceive thyself nor shall ye boast of thy attainment, nor, shall ye flaunt thy learning before the un-KNOWING ones.

Be ye as wise and silent as the Sphinx, for therein is HUMILITY, and humility is a subject which I shall speak on at a later time - so be ye as one prepared to receive it. There are none pure without humility and that is one of the steps of ATTAINMENT - be ye as one which has attained - let it be so.

Blest are they which have attained humility - be it so and let it be said that the greatest among thee are the humble. Be it so, BE IT SO and SELAH.

Be ye as one which hast attained this state, and ye shall be blest with all the virtue of love. I say deceive NOT thyself, for therein is the greatest of folly, I come that ye may know thyself - let it be so.

When I speak of 'mind' it is the part which is given unto thee of the Father - and thy free-will conditions that "Mind Stuff" which is endowed unto thee in its virgin purity - yet because of thy free will thou hast become lost in the world of darkness and the great maze of trees which has seemed unto thee as a great black forest!

Now I say, ye shall come out of the blackness of despair, for therein ye shall have thy memory restored unto thee, and then ye shall know no darkness and ye shall have all knowledge of thyself from the beginning - and ye shall have the law revealed unto thee which governs all the planets and the fullness of them. I say there shall be no mysteries unto thee, for this do I now come unto thee that it may be so - I say therein is wisdom and the law which is hidden shall be revealed unto thee.

Blest are they which do receive this freedom, and gift of the Father/Mother God. Let not thy preconceived opinions trip thee up; and come as one prepared to receive of the Father thy inheritance in full; Bring not a cup filled with thy own offal/ thy own corruption and filth for therein is the pity - for I say it is thy leg-irons - cut them away and cast them aside and be ye as a little child - clean and empty - void of all thy contamination - cleanse out the OLD and cast it off. Prepare thyself to put on the WEDDING GARMENT - for I say unto thee the Bridegroom cometh and make haste to meet him.

O, Blest is the Bride of the Bridegroom, for he shall claim her and great shall be their joy - so be it and SELAH. Berean.

Be Ye of One Mind

Beloved - Was it not said that one should be sent unto thee, and was it not done? Has it not been done? I say unto thee I have kept my word - yea, I have done greater, I have sent unto thee three, and are they not my servants? I say they are "My Servants" and they are brought for that "My Work" that My work might be accomplished in this the last day - I do say unto thee "THE LAST DAY" THE DAY OF THE LORD! When one shall go forth MIGHTY and STRONG - and this one shall proclaim his Sonship/ His Godhood and He shall be as one of God - come unto the Earth from the Etherial, wherein there is no darkness, wherein is nought but LOVE - for this does HE come that there might be LOVE among thee.

I say unto thee let there be unity and I say that there is nought within HIM which is come - save LOVE - for LOVE containeth nought save itself and love is contained within itself - for this is the "ALPHA, AND THE OMEGA" for therein is ALL that has been - ALL that ever shall be - which shall endure. ALL WISDOM, MERCY, JUSTICE, which is LOVE. I say unto thee - be ye as "ONE". This ONE COMMANDMENT do I give unto thee this day: this I say again! OH, ye Children, how many times have I said - "Be ye of one mind" and I have given unto thee from out my LOVE - from out My Store of

Wisdom, one which I have sent forth unto thee - that 'this thing' may be accomplished - that this the Father's PLAN may be brought forth in the completion, and in its fullness.

I say unto thee - thy work but beginneth, and mighty shall it be! I have said that I shall bring forth My Servants from out among them and I shall make of them "WISE MEN" and I shall make of them prophets in their own right - So be ye as ones prepared to bear witness of me and to bear testimony of these 'My Words" "My Works"! For this have I given unto thee this part - now I say unto thee I shall confound the "wise" and I shall justify the JUST, and I shall lift up the lowly and the humble, and I shall give unto them authority and power over the elements - and I shall be unto them that which they have need of.

Now I say unto thee "MIGHTY" is the word of Solen Aum Solen, speak it with reverence, as a HOLY BENEDICTION, keep it holy and immaculate and bless thyself with it by keeping it ever in thy heart - I AM with thee and I bless thee with MY BEING. I AM Sananda the Son of God.

Recorded by Sister Thedra of the Emerald Cross

One Mighty and Strong

Berean speaking unto thee: I say, Blessings be upon thee this day - go in peace and be at poise - and carry the Light unto them which know not that He, the Lord of Hosts is come - I say give unto them this my word that He, the Lord of Hosts, the "ONE MIGHTY AND STRONG" has come and He is within the Earth as flesh and bone: and He is as one made flesh that they may have Light more abundantly.

I say, that they may have LIGHT MORE ABUNDANTLY - So let it be. Be ye as my messenger unto them - give unto them as it is given unto thee for them - for I say unto them that they are walking in darkness and they know NOT the Great DIVINE PLAN which is NOW in operation - and he which THINKS himself wise is a traitor unto himself - for he shall be faced with his foolishness.

I say unto thee deceive not thyself - for I am in the place wherein there is no darkness and I see wherein is MUCH darkness and too, I say that ye are a sad lot for thy unknowing - Now ye shall be as ones blessed to be up and about the Father's business, and ye shall be as ones led into the place wherein ye shall be given the law governing the elements of the earth, and for that matter all law shall be revealed unto thee as ye are prepared for such revelation - which is given through the SONSHIP of God the Father - by VIRTUE of the SONSHIP - through thy preparation and thou alone art responsible for thy own preparation - yet as ye do prepare thyself, a legion of GOD'S servants shall come unto thy aid, and give unto thee assistance - each having a part to give unto thee - each a gift which shall be given as the time comes as ye are prepared to receive it.

Now I say unto thee which art my hands and my feet - that ye shall earn thy reward - for it is ever thus - for not ONE gift is added unto thine others before thou hast earned it - Let this be understood! THAT NOT ONE ACT, ONE DEED, ONE WORD, PASSES UNNOTICED, UNWEIGHED ON THE SCALES OF JUSTICE!

For justice weighs all thy acts, all thy words, deeds, in the scales of life - time - and I say that justice is the law of LOVE which includes all VIRTUE - all which is GOOD.

I say unto thee MY BRETHERN, be ye wise and learn this law, and be ye governed thereby and return unto thy abiding place even as ye went out from the Father - PURE - and ye shall be like unto HIM in perfection.

Bless the name of Solen Aum Solen - I AM His Son by His Grace Be ye the same BLESSINGS, BLESSINGS, IN HIS NAME.

ADOMNI SHELOHEIM -

Berean

> **Recorded by Sister Thedra of the Emerald Cross**

Seek Me Out!

Beloved of Mine Being: Say unto them in Mine Name that I am now among them for the purpose of bringing them out of bondage - and I say unto them: it is Mine part to see them as ones which have no light and as ones dissatisfied with their lot - and I say unto them: "Their wisdom is not sufficient unto their salvation - neither is their works" - and too I say unto them their works shall be unto me and their work shall be dedicated unto Me - and I shall prosper them - when it is come that there is famine in the land - and pestilence on every hand - and when the winds shall blow and the land shall be parched - and the fires shall burn the stubbles of the field and no water to quench it.

I say unto them: be ye mindful of me in thine days of prosperity - and I shall remember thee in the day of thine trials - for this do I say unto them: "Remember Me the Creator which hast given unto thee of Mine Mercy, Mine Love, Mine Wisdom that ye might have thine existence upon the Earth", and remember that this is the place for thine preparation, it is the "School of Melchizedek" it is the time: it is now come when ye shall receive that which hast been kept for thee ---

Now ye shall tell them as I would that there is none so sad as he which betrays himself, or his trust. And I say unto them, there are none so foolish as the one which thinks himself wise.

Now ye shall give unto them this word, for them which have ears - let them hear - for them which are of a mind to learn - let them come and be prepared for that which I have for them - so shall it profit them. I say unto them - be ye blest to learn of Me and for this I say: hear ye that which I say unto thee - and it shall profit thee much - so be it and Selah ---

While I say that Mine temple I have set upon a hill - and Mine Altar I have established, I say I shall bring them in as they art prepared - so shall it be. And too, I say they shall come with a clean heart and open hands - for they shall withhold nothing. They shall give their heart, their hands, their will - and surrender themself unto Me - and they shall remember no more the way of the dragon - they shall turn from him with distaste and they shall be no part of him - for I say unto them ye do not serve Me with one hand and the dragon with the other -- Ye give not lip service unto Me - while ye do his will - for I know thee for that which ye are. I am not deceived - neither do I hear thy words. I see thy light by which ye live!

I am the Lord thy God, think ye <u>not</u> to deceive Me - for I am not deceived. I have given unto thee the law sufficient unto thine preparation. <u>Now</u> ye shall apply it and live by it, and by so doing ye shall prepare thyself that ye might enter into Mine place of abode, and I say "None other enter herein." Be ye as one prepared - and for this shall I reveal Mine Self unto thee and for this do I say unto thee - "I walk amongst them while they know Me not" - for this do I say - seek Me out and I say I shall make Mine Self known unto thee: Yet, ye shall be as one prepared to receive Me - I am the Lord thy God - Sananda - Son of the Most High Living God - the Father Solen Aum Solen.

Recorded by Sister Thedra

The Power of Mine Light!

THE ALTAR:

By Mine own hand hast this Altar become manifest in the Earth, and few indeed shall come to know that which is done there upon: for I say I am now come that there be light in the Earth -- yet there is little for I have not expanded Mine light unto its fullness. I have not given unto them that which I am capable - for I say that it is as yet not come when they could endure it and when they could stand within the fullness of Mine light - for they have become accustomed to the darkness, and <u>they</u> <u>know</u> <u>not</u> <u>the</u> <u>power</u> <u>of</u> <u>Mine</u> <u>light</u>! I say they could not ENDURE IT - for it would be unto them great power which they could <u>not</u> ENDURE! While I say unto thee I know that which they can and I shall give unto them as they are prepared to receive - so be it <u>as</u> they are <u>prepared</u>. So shall they draw nigh unto Me - and I shall give unto them in part and as they grow in strength, I shall give unto them - for I say I give not unto Babes the power of the Ox, and I give not unto babes Mine pearls which know not the price thereof ---

Now - I have spoken unto them which have ears to hear and unto them let them hear - and them which have eyes let them see - for I speak unto thee of the Greater things which are to come when thou art prepared ---

Now I say: Arise thine sights: quicken thine steps - alert thine self and be ye as one prepared to take up thine arms and to go forth as into battle for I say unto thee there is a great and mighty work to be done - and it shall be accomplished with the light which is thine imperishable instruments of War - which rust not. I say Mine instruments rust not - neither do they vanish with time: yet they ever grow more bright - more triumph in the hands of the warriors of truth and justice - for these are Mine men - truly prepared - truly sent forth to slay the dragon. I say it shall be done. I say - Hail unto them - for I say none shall vanquish them: they shall return home the victor. They shall be as "one man" with "one Aim" - "one purpose". Oh mighty is the army and great the Conquest - for I say unto thee I go before thee that ye might be prepared for that which shall be done - for I am he which knows and I say unto thee I am the General in Chief of this Army - which shall march forth to conquer - and conquer they shall - and I say great shall be the Victory. I say hail unto the Victor!

Be ye at Peace --- Yet ye shall not rest upon thine laurels --- Yet ye shall be as one alert for the call hast gone out - Arise! Awaken all ye Nations - go forth in Mine Name. I say it shall be heard --- so be it Selah.

I am Sananda

Son of God

> **Recorded by Sister Thedra**

Prepare Thyself to Enter Other Worlds

"NOW IT IS COME WHEN THE DOORS OF OTHER WORLDS, OTHER REALMS, OTHER PLANETS, SHALL SWING WIDE BEFORE THEE. YET I SAY UNTO THEE: YE SHALL PREPARE THYSELF TO ENTER THEREIN; FOR NONE SHALL ENTER THEREIN UNPREPARED. AND FOR THAT HAS THE FATHER SEEN FIT TO GIVE UNTO THEE A NEW DISPENSATION...."

Seek Me Out

"WHILE I SAY THAT MINE TEMPLE I HAVE SET UPON A HILL AND MINE ALTAR I HAVE ESTABLISHED, I SAY I SHALL BRING THEM IN AS THEY ART PREPARED. SO SHALL IT BE. AND TOO, I SAY THEY SHALL COME WITH A CLEAN HEART AND OPEN HANDS: FOR THEY SHALL WITHHOLD NOTHING. THEY SHALL GIVE THEIR HEART, THEIR HANDS, THEIR WILL, AND SURRENDER THEMSELF UNTO ME. AND THEY SHALL REMEMBER NO MORE THE WAY OF THE DRAGON; THEY SHALL TURN FROM HIM WITH DISTASTE AND THEY SHALL BE NO PART OF HIM. FOR I SAY UNTO THEM: YE DO NOT SERVE ME WITH ONE HAND AND THE DRAGON WITH THE OTHER. YE GIVE NOT LIP SERVICE UNTO ME WHILE YE

DO HIS WILL; FOR I KNOW THEE FOR THAT WHICH YE ARE. I AM NOT DECEIVED; NEITHER DO I HEAR THY WORDS--I SEE THY LIGHT BY WHICH YE LIVE!

"I AM THE LORD THY GOD--THINK YE <u>NOT</u> TO DECEIVE ME; FOR I AM NOT DECEIVED. I HAVE GIVEN UNTO THEE THE LAW SUFFICIENT UNTO THINE PREPARATION. <u>NOW</u> YE SHALL APPLY IT AND LIVE BY IT; AND BY SO DOING, YE SHALL PREPARE THYSELF THAT YE MIGHT ENTER INTO MINE PLACE OF ABODE--AND I SAY NONE OTHER ENTER HEREIN. BE YE AS ONE PREPARED--AND FOR THIS SHALL I REVEAL MINE SELF UNTO THEE; AND FOR THIS DO I SAY UNTO THEE: I WALK AMONGST THEM WHILE THEY KNOW ME NOT. FOR THIS DO I SAY: SEEK ME OUT AND I SAY I SHALL MAKE MINE SELF KNOWN UNTO THEE: YET YE SHALL BE AS ONE PREPARED TO RECEIVE ME. I AM THE LORD THY GOD, SANANDA, SON OF THE MOST HIGH LIVING GOD."

"MANY ARE NOT ABLE AS YET TO RECEIVE OF THIS STRONG MEAT FOR YET ANOTHER AGE. THOSE WHO ARE READY MUST BE REACHED. NONE CAN BE LOST BECAUSE OF LACK OF OPPORTUNITY TO FIND THEIR WAY, OR HEED THE WARNING BEING SOUNDED FORTH FROM ALL THE FOUR CORNERS OF THE EARTH. IT MUST BE SENT FORTH UNTIL ALL HEAR AND EITHER ACCEPT OR DENY THE CALL TO FREEDOM."

Have I Not Returned?

"I GAVE UNTO THEE A COVENANT THAT 'I SHOULD GO AND PREPARE A PLACE FOR THEE'--AND RETURN THAT WHERE I GO THERE YE MIGHT GO ALSO. HAVE I NOT RETURNED? HAVE YE PREPARED THYSELF TO RETURN WITH ME? IT IS NOW COME WHEN MANY ARE HERE UPON EARTH WHICH COME EVEN AS I AM COME THAT YE MAY RETURN WITH ME. THIS IS THE DAY FOR WHICH YE HAVE WAITED."

I SHALL BE WITHIN THE EARTH BUT A SHORT WHILE.

"AND FOR THIS HAVE I COME INTO THE EARTH AT THIS TIME THAT I MIGHT FULFILL MY COVENANT WITH THEE, THAT WHERE I GO YE MAY ALSO GO. I SHALL BE WITHIN THE EARTH BUT A SHORT WHILE. AND I TOO SAY, THAT ALL WHICH ARE PREPARED TO RECEIVE ME SHALL BE CAUGHT UP WITH ME. FOR IT IS NOW COME WHEN MANY SHALL ASCEND UNTO THE FATHER EVEN AS I ASCENDED. I SAY FOR THIS HAVE I COME THAT YE MAY OVERCOME DEATH. SO BE IT AND SELAH.

"I AM NOW GIVING UNTO THEE THAT WHICH YE CAN COMPREHEND; SO SHALL YE BE QUICKENED AND YE SHALL KNOW AS I KNOW. SO BE IT AND SELAH. I AM ONE WHICH WAS KNOWN AS JESUS OF NAZARETH, NOW CALLED SANANDA, SON OF GOD."

This Is the <u>Last Time</u> I Shall Come

"I AM UNTO THEE I AM THE LORD THY GOD. HEAR YE ME AND REJOICE. THE DAY IS COME WHEN YE SHALL KNOW. I SAY YE SHALL KNOW; SO SHALL IT BE. I GO NOT OUT AGAIN. FOR I HAVE SAID UNTO THEE: NO MORE SHALL I GO INTO THE EARTH THAT THEY BE DELIVERED; FOR THIS IS THE <u>LAST TIME</u> I SHALL COME FOR THEIR SAKE. I SAY NO MORE SHALL THEY PUT THEIR FINGERS IN MINE WOUNDS FOR IT IS FINISHED. I SAY THEY SHALL SEEK ME OUT--THEN I SHALL SHOW UNTO THEM MINE FACE."

I Am Within the Body of Flesh, As Man

"GO INTO ALL THE WORLD AND PROCLAIM ME, AND SAY UNTO THEM IN MY NAME: I AM COME AND I SPEAK UNTO THEM AS MAN. AND I SAY: I AM COME. I AM WITHIN THE BODY OF FLESH, AS MAN; YET MY BODY BINDS ME NOT! I SAY I AM HERE, AND I SHALL GO UNTO ANY WHOSEVER, WHICH PREPARES HIMSELF TO RECEIVE ME. I SAY I SHALL GO UNTO ANYONE WHICHSOEVER, WHICH PREPARES HIMSELF FOR TO RECEIVE ME. HE SHALL BE AS ONE UNOPINIONATED: HE SHALL BE AS ONE WHICH HAS NO MALICE IN HIS HEART; HE SHALL BE AS ONE WHICH HAS A MIND TO RECEIVE ME. HE SHALL BE AS ONE MADE GLAD! FOR I COME THAT THEY MAY HAVE LIGHT. I BRING UNTO THEE GREAT LIGHT; AND WHEN IT IS COME THAT YE ARE PREPARED TO RECEIVE ME, YE SHALL BE STRONG ENOUGH TO ENDURE MY LIGHT."

Jesus Amongst Us?

"I SAY THEY WHICH ARE THE TRAILBLAZERS ARE THE ONES WHICH ARE THE HARDY OF SPIRIT - AND UNAFRAID OF THE CRUEL TONGUES OF MAN. I SAY PITY ARE THEY WHICH DO FEAR THE TONGUES OF MEN! I SAY THEY ARE THE SERVANTS OF THE DRAGON, AS THE ONES WITH THE VILE AND PITIFUL TONGUES. I SAY THAT THE ONES WHICH ARE FILLED WITH FEAR ARE THE TOOLS OF THE DRAGON. THEY ARE UNWITTINGLY USED FOR HIS PURPOSE; AND HE HAS CAUSED THEM TO FEAR. THEY ARE AFRAID OF LIGHT AND TRUTH; HENCE THEY TURN AWAY FROM THE LIGHT. HE, THE DRAGON, WHISPERS INTO THEIR EAR WHILE THEY SLEEP, AND SAYS UNTO THÉM, 'THIS IS NOT FOR THEE; IT IS STRANGE UNTO THEE. THIS IS NOT THE WAY OF THY FOREFATHERS; THEY HAD NOTHING OF THE LIKE. I SAY THEY HAD NO COMMUNICATION WITH GOD. THEY HAD NO COMMUNICATION WITH THE LORD, THE CHRIST. WHAT IS THIS THAT THEY SAY, JESUS AMONGST US? NAY NOT SO!'

"I SAY UNTO THEM: YE SLEEPERS! YE FOOLS! YE IDOLATORS! I SAY YE ARE BEFUDDLED. I SAY YE ARE ASLEEP. YE ARE AMONG THE WALKING DEAD. YE KNOW ME NOT! I SAY YE ARE AS ONES BEGUILED. AND YE ARE BOUND BY THY CREEDS, THY PRACTICES OF MAGIC, BY THY OPINIONS, AND BY THY LEG IRONS WHICH YE FORGE FOR THYSELF. I SAY UNTO THEE YE ARE HELD FAST BY THEM. I SAY I COME THAT YE MAY HAVE LIGHT--AND FREEDOM. BE YE NOT DECEIVED-- GOD IS NOT MOCKED. AND HE WHICH WOULD TRY IS THE GREATEST OF FOOLS.

"BE YE ALERT AND SING YE PRAISES UNTO HIM AND GIVE UNTO HIM THANKS THIS DAY IS COME. SPEAK WITH THEM WHICH HAVE EARS TO HEAR; I SPEAK WITH THEM WHICH INVITE ME IN. I AM NOT TO BE CALLED A FRAUD, NOR A LIAR. I SAY I AM IN THY MIDST, AND I SHALL MAKE MYSELF KNOWN WHEN YE HAVE PREPARED THYSELF FOR TO RECEIVE ME. AND I AM NOT DECEIVED.

I AM THE SON OF GOD, SANANDA, KNOWN AS THE NAZARINE."

Ye Shall Give unto Them This Word

"YE SHALL GIVE UNTO THEM THIS WORD AND IT SHALL GO FORTH TO BEAR WITNESS OF THAT WHICH I HAVE SAID UNTO THEE. AND THEY SHALL BE WISE TO ACCEPT THEE IN MY NAME. SO BE IT ALL WHICH RECEIVE ME AND THEY WHICH RECEIVE ME SHALL RECEIVE OF THE FATHER. SO BE IT AND SELAH.

"I SAY THEY WHICH DENY MY WORD DENY ME. THEY WHICH DENY ME DENY THE FATHER. I AM ONE WITH HIM AND I AM NOT TO BE DENIED; NEITHER ARE MY HANDS DENIED. I SAY I HAVE CALLED THEE FORTH. I HAVE SIBORED (TAUGHT) THEE WELL. I HAVE PLACED WITHIN THY HAND THE WORD. AND I HAVE GIVEN THEE THE AUTHORITY AND THE POWER TO BLESS THEM AS I WOULD BLESS THEM. I AM HE WHICH IS SENT THAT THEY MAY BE BLEST. I AM SANANDA, SON OF GOD, KNOWN AS JESUS THE

CHRIST. THE SON OF GOD AM I, BORN OF MARY, WARD OF JOSEPH. I AM KNOWN BY THE NAME OF SANANDA WITHIN THE TEMPLE OF LIGHT."

Not One Word is to Be Changed

SAY, YE SHALL SAY IT AS I HAVE GIVEN IT, AND NOT ONE WORD IS TO BE CHANGED; FOR IT IS GIVEN UNTO ME TO KNOW THAT WHICH I SAY; AND NO MAN SHALL BE UNTO ME CENSOR. FOR I AM GIVEN TO VOICE THAT WHICH I DO VOICE <u>FOR A PURPOSE</u> WHICH SHALL SERVE MY CAUSE.

"I AM NOT OF A MIND TO BE CENSORED; FOR I AM IN THE PLACE WHEREIN I AM FOR A PURPOSE. AND NO MAN SHALL STAY MY HAND; NOR SHALL HE GIVE ME THE DREGS OF HIS CUP. FOR IT IS NOT MY WAY TO GIVE UNTO MY OWN THAT WHICH WOULD BE TO HIM A STUMBLING BLOCK; AND YET THEY STUMBLE OVER MY PEARLS AND RECOGNIZE THEM NOT!

"I AM AS ONE PREPARED TO GIVE UNTO MY SERVANTS THEIR PART WHICH IS WISE AND PRUDENT. AND I AM NOT A FOOL. NOR AM BOUND BY ANY MAN'S PUNY THINKING OR HIS BELIEF; FOR I AM OF THE FATHER SENT AND I GIVE UNTO HIM AN ACCOUNT. AND I AM NOT OF A MIND TO ACCOUNT FOR MY ACTIONS AND MY WORDS TO ANY MAN."

I am Come that They Might be Free

"THE FATHER HAST WILLED THAT MAN RETURN UNTO HIS SOURCE FREE FROM ALL CONTAMINATION, FREE FROM ALL HIS LEGIRONS, FREE FROM ALL DARKNESS; AND TOO, I SAY I AM COME THAT THEY MIGHT BE FREE--EVEN AS I AM. I COME WITH A PURPOSE, AND WITH ONE PURPOSE--THAT MANKIND MIGHT BE FREE FROM ALL BONDAGE. SO BE IT I SHALL OFFER UNTO THEM MINE HAND, MINE SERVICE, MINE LOVE, MINE MERCY. AND UNTO ALL WHICH DOTH ACCEPT IT, I SAY UNTO THEM: 'COME YE AND FOLLOW YE ME, AND I SHALL LEAD THEE OUT OF BONDAGE.' SO SHALL IT BE; FOR MINE FATHER HAST SENT ME THAT IT BE SO.

"NOW WHILE I SAY UNTO THEE (THEDRA): YE SHALL GIVE UNTO THEM THESE WORDS THAT THEY MIGHT BE PREPARED TO RECEIVE ME AND OF ME; YET YE SHALL NOT TRESPASS UPON THEIR FREE WILL. FOR IT IS THEIRS--THEIR 'ONLY' POSSESSION. AND IT IS THEIRS TO CHOOSE WHICH WAY THEY GO. SO BE IT THAT THEY SHALL MAKE THEIR CHOICE. LET IT BE THEIRS--NOT THINE TO SAY!"

Be Ye as One Prepared to Receive Me

"NOW YE SHALL SAY UNTO THEM IN MINE NAME THAT I AM COME INTO THE EARTH AS A MAN. AND AS A MAN I WALK AMONG THEM, AND I SAY THAT I PASS AMONG THEM AS SUCH AND THEY KNOW ME NOT, SUCH IS THEIR

BLINDNESS. IT IS THE WAY OF THE FLESH; FOR I SAY THEY ARE BOUND IN FLESH, WHILE I AM NOT BOUND IN FLESH. I AM FLESH--YET I AM NOT FLESH; NEITHER IS FLESH ME; NEITHER AM I OF THE EARTH. I SAY I AM SENT OF THE FATHER--SENT THAT YE TOO MAY OVERCOME FLESH EVEN AS I. I SAY I HAVE OVERCOME FLESH; I HAVE OVERCOME DEATH. I HAVE COME TO GIVE UNTO THEE THE LAW; YET I SAY UNTO THEE, I GIVE NOT TO THE UNJUST AND THE IMPRUDENT. I SAY: FOR MINE PEARL WITHOUT PRICE THOU SHALT PREPARE THINE OWN SELF. NOW BE YE NOT DECEIVED; FOR I SAY UNTO THEE, YE ENTER NOT INTO MINE PLACE OF ABODE WITHOUT THE PROPER PREPARATION. NOW BE YE NOT SO FOOLISH AS TO THINK SO; FOR IT IS THAT FOR WHICH THOU DOST PREPARE THINE SELF. BE YE AS ONE PREPARED TO RECEIVE ME AND OF ME. FOR I HAVE SAID UNTO THEE, I SHALL COME AS A THIEF IN THE NIGHT, AND I SHALL FIND THEE EATING AND DRINKING AND IN THE PLACES WHERE IN THOU DOST SEEK TO GRATIFY THINE SENSES-THINE APPETITES. NOW I SAY YE SHALL BE AS ONES FOUND NAPPING; FOR I SAY I AM NOT OF A MIND TO WAIT. "

NO TIME TO WASTE!

I SAY, "THEY WHICH FOLLOW ME SHALL ABIDE WITHIN THE LIGHT WHICH NEVER FAILS--WHEREIN THERE IS NO SORROW. I SAY THIS IS THE DAY OF DECISIONS. WHEREIN HAVE I BEEN FOUND WANTING? HAVE I NOT KEPT MY COVENANT WITH THEM? HAVE I NOT PREPARED THE PLACE FOR THEM?

"NOW I AM RETURNED UNTO THEM; YET THEY KNOW ME NOT! I SAY PITY ARE THEY! FOR I FIND THEM SLEEPING; AND THEY ARE AS ONES SLEEPING THE SLEEP OF THE 'DEAD.' I SAY UNTO THEE, THEY ARE A SAD LOT! NOW YE SHALL BE UNTO THEM MY HANDS, MY VOICE, FOR THIS PART; AND THEY SHALL ACCEPT THEM FOR WHICH THEY ARE--OR, THEY SHALL BE CAUGHT UP SHORT. I SAY THEY SHALL BE CAUGHT NAPPING. NOW YE SHALL GIVE UNTO THEM THIS WORD, AND THEY SHALL BE REMINDED OF THESE MY WORDS WHEN IT IS COME THAT THEY ARE DISCOMFORTED. AND THEY SHALL BE AS ONES WHICH SHALL CALL OUT LORD! LORD! HAST THOU FORGOTTEN US? OR, THEY SHALL MAKE HASTE UNTO ME AND PREPARE THEMSELF TO RECEIVE ME AND OF ME. THEY SHALL BE DILIGENT IN THEIR SEARCH FOR ME."

"THE DAY OF DECISION IS COME; FOR THE TIME DRAWETH NIGH WHEN THEY SHALL BE FORCED WITH THE PART WHICH SHALL CALL FOR GREAT AND HASTY DECISION: FOR THERE SHALL BE NO TIME TO WASTE. THERE SHALL BE NO TIME TO WASTE! FOR TIME RUNS OUT!

AND THIS IS THE DAY LONG PROPHESIED; AND THEY KNOW NOT IT IS COME--HERE--NOW! BLAME NOT ANOTHER (I SAY UNTO THEM) FOR THY FRAILTIES: FOR THOU HAST HEARD THESE MY WORDS. FOR I AM NOT ALONE. I SAY I AM NOT ALONE! I HAVE COME WITH MANY OF MY BROTHERS FROM THE REALMS OF LIGHT THAT YE MAY KNOW THAT THERE IS A NEW DAY, A NEW DISPENSATION-- AND NEW LAWS NOW REVEALED WHICH YE HAVE NOT KNOWN. THIS IS MY DAY! SAYETH THE LORD GOD OF HOSTS. AND I AM HE. I HAVE SPOKEN--SO BE IT I SHALL SPEAK AGAIN AND AGAIN. I AM SANANDA."

* * *

Some clergymen have called their parishioners together, and it has been found that the most God-fearing and praying people among their members are the ones who have been taken from their midst. Many clergymen and priests are also among the vanished people. As a result of these events, a bishop in a large religious community has called clergymen under his authority to attend a meeting tonight.

By this time there had elapsed 3½ hours since the first report from Oslo, and events were proving that all the time new reports were arriving from countries all over the world with similar news concerning vanished people. From Korea in the Far East came the most sensational statement.

"In Korea, the number of vanished people is estimated at several hundred thousand, among them many military men from the United Forces,"

To describe occurrences as they increased during those first hours would be quite impossible. In the streets people were running to and fro wringing their hands, especially the mothers who had lost their children. A large number of people, however, were deriding and cursing both God and people. One man came running down the street wringing his hands and shouting: "Take care! Take care! We will soon all be taken!" Probably he had lost his reason.

An elderly woman stood in a corner with folded hands, looking up at the sky. She was saying: "Oh no, not when we were not prepared and ready to go with Him when He came. Probably no one will be taken from now on. Good Lord, Jesus, help us! Now it has happened! I have been religious all my life but I never believed it would happen in this way and that He was to come in actual fact. I never believed everything so literally."

From the railway it was announced that in spite of everything no accidents had occurred. Only one train was standing at Finse without its driver and guard. An order was sent to all station-staffs to search carefully along the whole track for people who could possibly have jumped off the eastbound train, meeting with an accident as a result. This was because several travelers had disappeared. From the fjords and coastal shipping also more reports were sent, again concerning people disappearing from their posts.

Next appeared a paragraph in the newspapers, exhorting the people to be considerate and calm. It stated that the police and authorities were working everywhere to obtain an accurate estimate of the total number of vanished people. Scientists, especially meteorologists, were also at work - trying desperately to find the cause of this remarkable phenomenon.

Subsequently a report from the U.S.A. arrived, stating that information was coming in from the police in Eastern Europe similar to the news already received in Norway. Details were also forthcoming about terrible traffic troubles in U.S.A., together with many traffic accidents. The newspapers stated that the next day they would be receiving more detailed reports concerning events in the U.S.A.

At 8 o'clock that evening a news broadcast informed the public that the catastrophe was apparent in the same form throughout the whole world. Up to this time most was known about large towns and cities, but reports were subsequently being sent in from all parts of the countryside. The radio report continued:

"Many people have completely vanished. In the southern part of the world similar things have happened and appear to be exactly parallel with what we have seen here in Norway."

A horrible anxiety was by now ruling everywhere. It seemed as though people dared not go to bed on this terrible night. In the streets hysterical discussions took place and more and more the opinion was growing that the mystery had to do with Christians and Christianity. Those who had known the vanished people stated that it was only those they had deemed Christian fanatics and innocent children who had been taken away.

A brewery worker was known to have said: "Yes! Hans Olsen is gone now, and probably it is what he used to preach about here. He always said Jesus was to come and fetch him!"

"Yes," replied another, "We had someone like that, and he's gone, too. Now I suppose the authorities will have to forbid all religion so such a thing can't happen again."

"Ah, no!" exclaimed a third. "It will never occur again. Doubtless these Christians were right, for they had a premonition about it. If we'd only listened to them perhaps it would have been better for us than to have to live in this hell and chaos that is breaking over us now, and will probably get worse."

"So you believed in them?" someone else added. "Then you ought to have gone with them when they went!"

"I wish I had been able to do that," answered the other, as he turned to go on his way. One of the listeners called after him:

"You should be hanged, both you and all other people who concern themselves with this feebleminded Christianity!"

The following day, the newspapers could not give any explanation of the mystery, which remained obstinately unsolved, while from every country in the world reports continued to pour into news centers. From missionary stations it was reported that many Christian people had disappeared and that only a small number of Christians were left behind.

At the meeting called by the bishop quite a number of priests and clergymen proved to be present, although many of their erstwhile colleagues had also been carried away. A nervous and dismal atmosphere prevailed throughout the assembled people. A report on the meeting stated that many were very unhappy, but there was no doubt in anyone's mind that what had happened was the "rapture of the

Christian Church," or, as some people had called the forthcoming event, "The Fetching of the Bride of Christ."

Some clergymen at the meeting confessed that in spite of their theological training and studies of the Bible, they had never believed it would happen in this way. Neither had they ever heard of regeneration. One young clergyman stated:

"I have never been taught in such a way. The professors didn't speak of the possibility of such a thing happening in these days!"

There was a tendency to discussion, but minds were too disturbed for such talk to be matter of fact. This was commented upon by a journalist reporting on the meeting. Subsequently, a report based on the findings of the meeting was drawn up, which the police proposed to lay before the public to test their opinion. Most of those participating at the meeting were agreed on the contents, which were presented in these terms:

"What has happened was a predicted Biblical event, the so-called "Rapture of the Christian Church," or, "Return of Christ for His Bride," which meant that Christ had taken His people from the earth. At present this was all that could be said."

The police proved uneasy about presenting such a statement to the public, thinking it was the product of a nervous and hysterical imagination. Also, they felt that the matter was of so far-reaching a nature that it should be dealt with at Government level. If, in fact, it proved to have anything to do with the Christian religion, perhaps all churches and religious houses ought to be closed until a better view of events had been obtained and the affair clarified. This being an international problem, perhaps there should be a common attitude to the affair. Perhaps the U.N. would take charge and examine the problem thoroughly.

Among the Christians, the atmosphere seemed to be very pressing and heavy. On the first Sunday after the disappearance of the people all churches and meeting places were full to capacity. In some churches there was no minister, and many of the erstwhile members were reported to have disappeared. In others there was a sprinkling of believing people left, but in addition there was an enormous stream of outsiders who had, in most cases, met with "the great accident," as they termed it.

People were desirous of hearing God's word, but now it was obscured. Someone tried to read from the Bible, but after a brief attempt he said: "I don't understand anything." The Bible was handed to another, but he said, "I can't read it!" Other people wept. The majority seemed to be united about Christianity being the direct cause of this tragic event, and they had thought they could obtain a possible explanation of this thing at Christian places of worship. Many me to seek God's help. They were profoundly unhappy.

At most meetings there was total confusion. At one, a man stood with clenched fists and cried to the clergyman: "It's your fault that so many of us have been left! You never told us that Jesus was to return to fetch His people, and still less about having a pure heart, being filled with the Holy Ghost and having everything straight with God and our fellow men! I know what has held <u>me</u> back! Small things, yes, small things, but... but, God help me!"

"Be silent!" said the clergyman. He considered he had done his duty.

Thus it went on, one person blaming another, intermingled with roaring and crying. They were knocking, but the door was closed!

The state of growing panic can hardly be described. People realized that a terrible time was to come. All hope had gone. The gate was irrevocably closed. They knocked and cried - all those who had been content with empty Christian words. Some had professed Christianity for the sake of fellowship; others only because they had had different tasks as choir members and in the music section. Still they had been without regeneration, without the adoption of Sons, and by that the right also of the inheritance of God given through Jesus Christ. Indeed, for many the life they had led as members of church congregations was no different from taking part in any section of society's activities; a hobby to help leisure time go faster. But now they all knocked at the door crying, "My Lord! My Lord, open the door to me!"

In addition to all this, horrible rumors began to circulate that the Third World War was liable to break out at any moment. Diplomatic relations between East and West were broken off. Terror grew.

Concerning the taking of Christ's Church from the earth and what to do about Christian people, it took the authorities short time to reach a decision. From the Eastern states an edict was issued to the effect that the communist states now were at the head of everything, and that all Christian activity and meetings now were forbidden by law. This was accompanied by threats of the death penalty, and the mention of the name of Jesus Christ was also forbidden. Countries were to be completely purged of Christian literature. With the Bible uppermost, everything was to be burnt. To have anything which in any way related to the Christian religion meant death to the owner.

In the Western States it took a somewhat longer time before such prohibitions were brought into force. But the Godless members of the people, both among the authorities and the common people, were shocked over what had happened and demanded that something drastic should be done. The majority won, and since Christianity was stated to be the cause of the accidents to the community, the result was in no doubt.

Thus the most terrible time in the history of mankind began. A great number of the Christian people left went on crying to God, refusing to obey the prohibitions. They were promptly arrested and examined under Gestapo conditions. "If you want to save your life, curse and deny Jesus Christ!" was the appalling statement.

In spite of this horror, thousands of people stood firm, and the wholesale murdering which followed was indescribable. Many victims were tormented until they died. There was no true law and order any more: SATAN WAS LET LOOSE. WOE TO THE WORLD, AND THEY WHO LIVE ON IT!

Several people yielded during this terrible pressure. They had no place to which they could flee, and the Scripture was being fulfilled, that "the whole earth is in the mercy of the wicked one." All countries were now united in their opinion about the extermination of Christians and Christianity. The prince of this world had now taken his power. Children betrayed their parents to their deaths.

Thus was fulfilled that which is written in the Gospel of Luke, Chapter 21:16, "AND THEY SHALL BE BETRAYED BOTH BY PARENTS AND BRETHERN AND KINSFOLKS AND FRIENDS; AND SOME OF YOU SHALL THEY CAUSE TO BE PUT TO DEATH... AND YE SHALL BE HATED OF ALL MEN FOR MY NAME'S SAKE."

Such a situation would appear impossible to describe, but God has given us knowledge of the whole thing in the Book of Revelation. The cry of the unhappy people left on the earth was: "Lord! Make these days shorter!"

My dear friend! You ought not to risk being left when Jesus comes to fetch His people, but you can know what to do about it. Go to God in prayer and ask for light and grace. Today there is time. Today you can be sealed as the property of Jesus Christ, and will be numbered among His people when He returns to fetch them.

For other new age scripts and prophecies write to the above address.

ON FOOD:

Beat the pores and cast no portion unto the food. For I have given no thought for what I eat. Give the best of thy fortune not to food - and not to the pore part of thee.

That which I eat I fret not for. I am a portion unto myself - and not unto the food.

I eat not of that which has been killed, and I eat not that which has been forgotten and let rot, for I am a particular person - and not any place can I find a funnier one than I, for I am not particular, yet I am, and when I have said I eat of nothing which has been killed, I eat of the fresh garden which has been plucked and killed.

Yet, it has not the former pain to remember. And I have given no thought to my food. Yet, I give my utmost care for it and the preparation of it. Yet, it burdens me not. And I have been no part of my food, yet, it becomes a part of me.

And as I am the Master - food bothers me not. Beleis.

ON PAIN:

Pain is the portion that the pores have portioned for themselves. The positive knows no pain, the positive knows only peace.

And forget the pores, and the spores, and their pain, I say unto you the PEACE I bring knows no pain - and my peace is upon thee. Beleis.

ON PEACE:

Peace is my part of thee, and no place can I see the pores who have my Peace.

And fortunes have I put at their command, but they squander them on the pore part of themselves.

And the Peace which I would give them they sell for the potters* fee. And wherein have I said unto thee that there shall be no Peace among them.

Fortunes have they of their own inheritance, and fortunes I have, but they know not my Father, and receive not any portion of my inheritance - therefore their fortunes know no part of my Peace, which is a princely inheritance.

Be aware of them - but partake not of their fortunes, for it availeth them nought but misery and want - foolish beings they!

For there is no fool so great as one who has given away his birthright! Beleis. *Undertaker

ON FRIENDSHIPS:

Because of friendships has the poor Red Star Earth been a better place and because of friendships has there been a fraternity of brotherhood which could not have existed without friendship.

Friends are the foundation for the Unity of Mankind - which begets Brotherhood such as the Brotherhood of which I am a member - and as I have told you, I am not a poor member. I give of my friendship unto all who seek it. Be unto me and my Brothers a fellow member - and forget not thy pledge - and swear allegiance to no pore - for I am the porter and I am the portal. Beleis.

ON DISAPPOINTMENTS:

Be a person who can say there is no disappointments - for I have told thee that there is no future - only the eternal NOW, and why should there be any plans for the future.

Bless the NOW! and live it to the full - and to the highest and noblest of thy stature and fret not about thy future. And as each day becomes the NOW - wherein is there a future? Forever and ever is NOW!

And wherein have I said there is a time for the only time is NOW! And foresee thy future as NOW! And bless this moment and our communion and be it such that profiteth thee. Beleis.

ON IMAGINATION:

Begin thy imaging with a drop of dew - and enlarge it unto an ocean and begin the ocean with the Cosmos and there is an organism within that ocean of Cosmic energy - and that is man in the Red Star. And his imaging has begot him his pores and spores - his torments and his pleasures and his pain, his imaging have destroyed or saved him.

Be a person who can image to perfection and peace - and unto the Creator of the things which are eternal that pass not away, or rust within the junkyards.

Beware of thy imaging and image the things you desire to have manifest unto the seen world for they do you know. Beleis.

ON LOYALTY:

This is no small part of friendship for I am the part of loyalty which has been taught me by my Father and Mother - for they have been unto me no poor part of loyalty and whereupon have I said they have been loyal?

There is no method to improve upon loyalty! It is of the essence and that essence is unto thy own self be true and to no man you can be false. For I am unto you the teacher of such sobrieties and my loyalty exceeds my patience and that is another lesson. Beleis.

ON PATIENCE:

This is a Virtue and no Virtue exceeds that of another for there are many and without one - Virtue is a static and not a positive for it is the force which motivates the being which becomes the Virtues and not any can be omitted and be unto the whole a Virtue.

Be upon the port whole and full of Virtue and no person can put the porter out. Beleis.

ON SIN:

Sin, my darling, is a poor part of knowledge - and a place within thy beam where knowledge is not! And without thy knowing there is distortion of facts. Blame not the sinner, and forgive him his distortion; forgive him his lack of facts. Be unto him a lamp yet cast no shadows before it. And be unto him a beacon, yet porter not his pores - for he has his own port to porter. Beleis.

ON VISITORS:

Visitors are ones who come for communion each with the other - or those who come for a purpose which they reveal not to the hostess - and be unto them most gracious. As each has come for his purpose -

give him his penny and say no port is out of place and call no pore an intruder, and enlighten him according to his capacity and fret not, for thy part has been established and I am thy fortune and thy doorkeeper. Beleis.

ON DUTY:

Duty is the portion that one establishes unto himself - and this follows loyalty as they follow unto the place which has been established by thy own source and from which thou has been sent out. And it is a connecting Link with thy source.

There is no sense of loyalty unto any other than thy own source and being. From this time forward it is the Oneness and no beginning and no end - and to this Oneness of being be loyal - no place is there a division. No place are there many or few. Just the eternal Oneness of thy Being. Beleis.

ON DAY:

Day is but that which seems light - and that which is not dark - and that which you see as light is but a time frame reference.

But as a flyer flies with the sun is as day, and as day is but an illusion unto the one who stands still there is but night and day unto his fortunes - but unto the flyer who travels with the light there is no night. Beleis.

ON NIGHT:

Whereupon have I told you of night for to them who have no fortune unto the light there is only night, and no place is there night unto the one who sees no night.

Be gone to thy spore when it is day - there will be no night -

And forget there has been a night. Forgive thy fortunes garnered unto the night. Beleis.

ON HOPE:

Hope is but a poor part of reality and nowhere did I say that I would teach you of hope, for that is not my mission to teach of hope. I come to teach you knowing and that availeth you the fortunes of which I have been speaking, and that is your inheritance from the Father.

Brag not of thy fortunes but be thou a fortune unto my teaching and know wherein thy treasure lies. Beleis.

ON UNDERSTANDING:

Understanding bringeth much wealth and the place wherein I am is peopled with those who understand thy weakness, and thy porters are not among them for they have gone to thy port and no place can they be found. And they are in the ports of those who have no understanding of the laws of which I teach - and they put forth their will and their might for a cause they think to be the right one. Yet, the other puts his forth and there is a clash of ideologies and a fortune lost, and no man understands the reason -

Be a person who can see the reason and not the results of the misunderstandings - and the frailties of the poor in spirit. Be gone to the business of understanding the cause of misunderstanding - which is the negative. And the positive is understanding and that is from another standpoint or point of reference. And no part of the unconscious part of the great forces which are at work to beset the peace of the Earth. Beleis.

ON SECRETS:

Secrets have I, but secrets have you none, and my secrets are not to be plundered but by thy time - I shall be unto you a revealer of mine in the time which is allotted to such things, I shall give of my treasure trove; and be unto you a porter and wherein have I said I have not told you secrets; but my secrets are no longer secret after I have revealed them to thee so be as wise as a serpent and silent as a sphinx. Beleis.

ON REVELATION:

Revelation is the portion which I have prepared thee. For I have since the beginning portioned out thy lot. And as thou has squandered it or valued it - have you coined thy tonnage - and what has thy tonnage been? A portion have I given unto thee of much value and my pearls I give not to babes - and I have revealed my prospectus to thee. This is revelation. Beleis.

ON TEACHERS:

Thy portion has been given for thee and for no students - but by thy lamp shall they walk thereby. And this is my lamp - carry it high and cast no shadow before it, and when I have told thee the things I have told thee, they are for thy enlightenment - and by thy own enlightenment - thou shall use wisdom in the portions thou giveth to the students and be in no hurry to give them the portions which are not for them. Beleis.

ON JUDGEMENT:

Judgement is the part which belongs to no part of thee and no part of me - for judgement is for each man to be his own and as he stands before himself as a naked boarder of his own house he shall see himself as he is, and by his own deeds shall he judge himself, and for himself he cannot become the personality he is not, and there is but one judge that is the law and the law must be balanced. Beleis.

ON BALANCE:

Balance is a law and that law must be served and the Father is the author of that law - and no man is exempt from the law of balance.

Thus is it ever striving to become balanced - there is no inequality in nature only an imbalance, and as the scales are balanced there is harmony. Unhappiness is a striving for balance, and sickness is an imbalance of the law, and harmony being that of balance. Laughter and tears are the laws of balance. Beleis.

ON INNOCENCE:

Ponder my words - there are none innocent - and none pure upon thy earth, for were they, they would not be there. For there is a laboratory, and that laboratory is the earth wherein are my experimenters, who are returning the hard route - and by their labors they are known to the few, who have become the initiated and by their fortunes have they paid the price for their admittance into another laboratory - which is my portion of their inheritance - and no place have they saved for me - but they have set up idols unto the scientists, and they have belittled the powers which they have plundered.

And when they have been stripped of their gadgets they are at a loss to know which is which! And when I have failed to look unto their gadgets for the part that they have given unto me, they call me unjust - these are the innocent and who has said that I am unjust? Beleis.

ON THE INNER CIRCLE:

The inner circle are those who are the ones who have been tried - and been found worth the processing and worth the admitting unto the whole, for the benefit of the whole - and not a single unit - for the sake of a few.

And when these have been found worthy there stands the princely crowd to assist with the ones who do qualify for admittance and none who qualify are sent away - there are none who have come without sanction by the whole of the inner circle. And by their own passports are they known - yet they carry no passports, or portfolio. Beleis.

ON WORK:

Work is the portion I have given thee and it can be a joy forever - and bless the work which I have portioned out to thee.

But be no part of the drudgery for I have not given thee drudgery - and I am thy timekeeper and no time have I for drudgery. So, keep my portion that I have given unto thee, and put not thy foot into a hole. Beleis.

ON RESPONSIBILITY:

Responsibility is given unto the wise and the prudent - and forget not thy wisdom which I have forched upon thee - for I have given thee of my learning and that is thy inheritance. So be wise as a serpent and silent as a sphinx.

But be thou a positive and the negative shall be no part of my wisdom, for I am both positive and negative and I am made whole. Be unto me a pointer and no man shall keep my keys - for I am the keeper. Beleis.

ON MAN AND WOMAN:

Bless them, and be it such that they marry and divorce, and try to find happiness.

But for this the pores are the better pores - and in no wise are they happier - the experiences are but the parts through which they learn that there is no place wherein they can find happiness in the negative but to be a positive, and to be a positive to the negative is to be whole - and no negative is without a positive but the negative is in the seen and the positive in the unseen and the positive is the keeper of the negative.

And my place is in the positive I am unto the negative and the positive.

But the negatives are not the masters, for they are not whole, and as my negative you write. As you write the written words are the negative, and the spoken words are the positive. The person who speaks is the positive to the spoken word and man is the negative to the positive which he does not see. So woman is the positive to the male and the male is the positive to the pore - and thus is the balance established. Beleis.

ON WISDOM:

Wisdom is the better part of knowing; whereupon thy knowing has failed thee thy wisdom has served thee. And no wisdom is so great that there is not more light to be gleaned - from that which you call experience.

And that which you call wisdom is but the idiot's delight - compared to the Father's words which shall be revealed in all their purpose. Forget not that this is but the beginning of thy learning - and no part of wisdom. It has been forched upon thee by me. And no wise man has the wisdom of the Father. From the beginning have you sought wise men - but they are but the ones who seek to be wise as thyself - and wherein have I said there are no wise save through the Father.

Be sought by the Father and receive thy inheritance. Beleis.

Recorded by Sister Thedra

The Last Enemy

"The last enemy that shall be destroyed is death". - Saint Paul.

In wandering away from the encampment I must have gone farther than I supposed, for presently I saw I was alone, with nothing but the wide, sad prospect of Judean Hills about me. Deep down on the left side the leaden gleam of the Dead Sea at the base of the mountains of Moab gave the only relief to the eye in this world of dull gray bareness.

I was about to return to camp when at a distance of perhaps twenty yards I saw ashes and refuse marking the spot where some band of nomads had recently pitched their tents. It was a natural impulse to go the necessary few steps onward, even though the ashes and refuse would be the only reward for my curiosity.

This was so nearly the cast that after a few minutes' idle inspection I was turning away, when suddenly my attention was caught by what I took to be a stone of peculiar formation. Gray on gray, it lay unobtrusively, a stick of stone, some eight inches long, and three or four in circumference. Countless ages of attrition, I was beginning to say to myself, must have been needed to wear it away to this smoothness and straightness, till I remembered that here on this hilltop which the sea had not reached for millions of years, no such attrition had been possible. To have taken this evenness of form it must have been worked on by the hand of Moab.

On going down the gentle slope, for it lay just below me, I saw that it was not a stone, but a leaden cylinder. Wedged into seam in the rock it had neither fallen there by accident nor been cast aside by someone impatient of task of carrying it about. Looking carefully around me to make sure I was not the victim of a plot, I dislodged it with some force, finding it light enough and small enough to go in a large pocket. Then I went back to camp.

What the cylinder contained I could only guess, having no immediate opportunity of definitely finding out. In the camp all my actions were subject to observation of the dragoman and his servants. If I were seen opening a cylinder obviously ancient, and not without some value in itself even if it were empty, I should be suspected. The thing might easily be some lost object of veneration, known throughout the series of tribes whose relations with one another are always mysterious to outsiders. At any rate, I ran no risk. The cylinder did not leave my person till I reached the safety of a hotel bedroom in Damascus.

It proved then to contain what I suspected, a parchment manuscript. I could see that the writing was in Latin, but beyond this elementary fact I had no knowledge. Impressively old it seemed to me, worn at the edges, and yet for the part intact.

The writing was in a flowing hand, with concentrations and little flourishes. No learning that I possessed threw any light on the things HISTORIC value. The cylinder itself seemed to be faintly engraved with a Byzantine conception of the Risen Christ, RUBBED DOWN BY THE HANDLING OF MANY generations.

But it chanced on the voyage from Beyruth to Marseilles. I fell in with a man I had known a few years earlier in the capacity of exchange, French Professor at Harvard. Renewing the old acquaintanceship, I became confidential on the subject of my "find". As, however, his field was philosophy, his opinion on the document of which he could decipher no more than isolated words, was not more expert than my own. On the other hand, he gave me an introduction to a colleague at the University of Montpellier, whose specialty was precisely in the reading and appraising of all kinds of ancient scripts.

In the end I received from him three or four expressions of opinions, of which one was his own, and the others of scholars in the same line of work. All agreed that this narrative given in the text was that of a genuine experience, though judgements differed as to whether or not the version in the cylinder was original. Three out of four declared it to be a very ancient manuscript of the latter half of the First Christion century.

In the question of the date I was personally interested in that of alone authenticity. To have a few pages torn from one of those lives which must have touched incidentally that of Jesus Christ, struck me as far more important than that the parchment and ink, or that the hand that used them, should have belonged to this year or to that. A copy was good enough for me, so long as I could feel that actual facts had been transmitted.

As to that the experts seemed to be agreed. Someone named Galba, of Roman family, though born at Tiberias on the Sea of Galilee, had in middle or old age written down what he remembered of his intercourse during boyhood with a wondrous personality, living then in Britean, and bearing the name of Jesus of Capernaum, as he commonly calls

Him, proclaimed as the founder of a new religion, he sets down for his children and grandchildren the memories he has treasured all of his life. He seems not to have been a Christian in the accepted sense of the term, nor to have known till shortly before writing that his own recollections of the Wondrous Personality had become a tradition for others. In the formation of the infant Christian Church he had no part, learning of its existence only after years of vicissitude in the outlying parts of the empire.

As to the story of the manuscript itself we had nothing to go on but surmise. Apparently by the fourth Christian Century it was recognized by its owner as a priceless possession. The cylinder had been then made for its protection. The faint engraving of the Risen Christ, with a still fainter background of a line of cypresses, was not later than Justian & Theodora.

It might easily have been the treasure of some monastery, of some princely house, till the looting of the Empire after the conquest by the Turks destroyed such objects, or scattered them. None the less this particular relic would seem to have been guarded with much care, perhaps with some superstition, as a talisman secret and sanctified. It had probably not been thrown away in the place where I had found it, but dropped in hasty breaking of camp.

The translation made for me in Montpellier was of course in French. My English translation of this French translation loses, I am told, most of the antiquity of thought and expression so naive in the original. I have only to add that as in the script there is neither punctuation, sentence, nor paragraph, these have been added by myself.

For several lines at the beginning only scattered words are legible.

father....

stone....

Toberias....

baths....

never....

architecture....

workman....

Italian....

From the text as it goes on we gather that what had been written was to the effect that the author's father had been an Italian stone mason, brought to Tiberias at the time of the building of the sumptuous baths in the foreign style erected there by the Herods. For this task workmen could not be found in Galilee, the Hebrews never having developed an architecture of their own beyond what met the simplest necessities.

It was well known to the historians that in building those cities of Gentile magnificence, Tiberias and Ceasarea Philipp, the Herods those cities of Gentile magnificence had been obliged to bring artisans from Tyre, Sodom, Egypt, Greece, and Italy - young Galba's father being one of them.

From further fragments of sentences we learned that the lad had been born at Tiberias, and had been left an orphan while still very young, a Gentile orphan in a land so hostile to Gentiles of any age that even helplessness stirred no pity. Almost as long as he could remember the child had been an outcast, living by his wits.

In the Jews' country of Galilee", he writes, "this was no great hardship. For the support of life little is required, and little they ever have had. Their houses are simple, and from our Italian point of view, flimsily constructed. Low, square and flat, they rarely consist of more than single rooms with a mat, a chest and a few earthen pots for the furnishings. Even for the Galileans this would be too wretched were it not for the roof on which most seasons of rain or storm, while from the roof to the fields or the orchards the transition is not great. In my boyhood I slept where night overtook me.

The climate being soft and sweet, it was seldom cold. Of clothing and food we required little. That little could be begged or stolen. I, Galba, was mostly obliged to steal, for when they knew I was a gentile boy they drove me from their doors, True, I could often deceive in this respect, being as proficient in the Jews' language as any son of their own; but they judged me by my countenance. The Jew's land of Galilee harboring many Gentiles, the housewives are suspicious of those who spoke their own tongue.

But, sleeping in the fields, eating when food chanced to come my way, drinking of the brooks, and wearing the garments more favored boys had cast aside as too ragged to cover nakedness, I contrived to live, from town to town, around the Sea of Galilee, I wandered, sometimes earning a few pence, but more often finding food and shelter as the birds and foxes do.

Being then about twelve years old, that from which I suffered most was the lack of love. Other boys had homes, parents, brothers, playmates, schools. I, Galba had nothing. If I ventured to join in a game being played in the market place, the lads of the town stoned me. If I drew near to a school, the teacher drove me thence. If in some vineyard or olive garden I found work, I was beaten, and often denied my pay when it became known that I was of Gentile parentage. Lying in the fields at night, I wept from anger and loneliness.

And when, as I saw nothing but hatred and contempt, I grew to hate and despise everyone -- my Hope was one day to be big and strong, so I might do ill to those who had done ill to me. When any such opportunity came to me I wrought as I could. I would rise at night to break the branches of the olive trees or pull up the shoots of grain.

Then I passed on, putting myself beyond detection before sunrise. When I found children feebler than myself I evil treated them, snatching their food and leaving them in tears. With older and stronger lads I frequently did battle, rending their garments and bruising their features, regretting only that I had no means of killing them. All this I did to be revenged, yet finding in my vengeance but small consolation.

Then it chanced that roaming one day between two towns I saw a multitude of men and women streaming from one of the cities and making their way up a mountainside. I listened to what was said to one another, so I learned that they were on the way to hearken to the words of one Jesus of Capernaum. Of this man I had heard much, some saying that He was a deceiver; some that He was a prophet; while all agreed that by the help of either God Saben the dispute was to which - He worked great cures and wonders.

Having nothing better to do I hung on the outskirts of the throng, recking little of the curses to which I was inured, and hoping to see a miracle. Of those who journeyed with me I gathered that this was also the chief motive, tho some seemed to be His disciples. As for me, Galba, I had little thought beyond curiosity, with the possible chance of picking up some article dropped by accident, or by filching a little food.

Later, as I skirted the seated throng looking for the place from which I was least likely to be driven, I heard a voice of which the very tones caused me to stand still. Loving and commanding at once, it was strong with the strength which penetrates, and makes every syllable distinct. Accustomed as I was to the raucous Galilean dialect, it was a strange new wonder in itself to perceive that there could be anything so sweet in human speech.

Never man like this man. As it is among the many things to be regretted that we know no way by which to preserve the sound of a voice, so we have language by which to convey its beauty to one who has not heard it. When I have said that this voice was music, I have still said nothing to express its entrancing qualities. Tho at first I saw not the speaker, He seemed to have seen me, and among all that throng, to be addressing me.

But I tell you who hear me, Love your enemies; treat those that hate you well; bless those who curse you; pray for those who abuse you".

In one of my bitterness of spirit, those words came like balm, soothing that hatred which was poisoning my life. A child of twelve has no impulse to hate. Love is the meat he thrives on, and the air he knows how to breathe. The thought that I could love those who hated me came to my oppressed young soul like relief from a madness within me.

In among the multitude I thrust myself till at last I saw Him. No more than I could give you the sound of His voice can I tell you what

He was like. The memory which remains with me is that of power and graciousness. Never have I seen elsewhere such capacity to overawe crowds and stand alone. Never was anyone so strong, and yet so winning and courageous. I have heard Him spoken of as grave, sorrowful, austere but of this I never saw anything. In my knowledge of Him, He was the embodiment of happiness. He inspired courage; health, sanity. Energy emanated from Him as youth and activity did likewise. You could not come into His Presence without the conviction that here was the form of perfect joy in which your own conditions, however afflicting, must be amended.

These thoughts I could not have had as a boy; they come to me in later life as an explanation. All I was capable of seeing at the time was that here was someone who would not turn me away. He might even love me. Already I loved Him. My instinctive purpose was to reach Him.

But in this I was hindered by the multitude. They held me back as one who has no right; they closed up their ranks against me so that I could not descend. He, himself was seated on a mound, a little hollow beyond which rose a series of natural turf-covered ridges like the seats in an amphitheater. As, in spite of all obstruction, I forced my way to the bottom, someone pushed me angrily and I stumbled forward. Thus I came into His Presence with a cry, a sorry lad, frightened, friendless and dirty with hot tears streaming from my eyes.

At my cry He interrupted His discourse to look at me where I lay in my shame. All fear was that He would rebuke me, but when in terror I lifted my eyes He only smiled. With a movement of His left arm, He made me understand that close by His side there was a place for me. "Come here". "But I could not move. 'Master', I moaned, 'I dare not. I am but a Gentile and an outcast.' "The sweetness of His smile played over me like sunlight. 'In the Kingdom of Heaven', He answered, 'there is neither outcast nor Gentile, but only the child of my Father.'

But Master, some among the crowd protested, 'the boy is a thief, known as a rogue and a vagabond in all our towns.'

When he has a home', came the reply, 'he will be so no longer,' To me He added: 'Your home is in the Father's House. Come.'

As a poor dog creeps, I crept to Him. Throwing His arm about my shoulder, He went on with His discourse. He seemed to be telling of the Kingdom of Heaven. The words themselves I did not understand. I recalled not that I listened. Merely to sit beside Him, within the refuge of His arms, was all the bliss I could ask. Never before that I could remember had my child's weakness known the solace of protection.

But presently I heard Him speaking words which, like those I heard on arriving, seemed specially addressed to me. Now and then, at certain points, He pressed me to Him more closely, as to summon my attention.

No slave can belong to two masters, he will either hate one and love the other, stand by one and make light of the other. You cannot serve God and Money. Therefore, I tell you not to worry about wondering what you will have to eat or drink, or about your body, what you will have to wear. Is not life more important than food, the body than clothes? Look at the wild birds. They do not sow or reap, or store food in the barns, and yet your Heavenly Father feeds them. Are you not of more account than they? But which of you with all of his worry can add a single hour to life? Why should you worry about your clothing? See how the wild flowers grow. They do not toil or spin, and yet I tell you, even Solomon in all his splendor was not dressed like one of them. But, if God beautifully dresses the wild grass, which is alive today and is thrown into the furnace tomorrow, will He not more surely clothe you? You who have so little faith do not worry and say, 'what shall we have to eat? or what shall we have to drink? or what shall we have to wear?' For these are all things the heathen are in pursuit of. But you must make His Kingdom and uprightness before Him your greatest care, and you will have all these other things besides.'

When He had finished He stood up, the whole multitude rising too. Many who were sick came begging Him to heal them while those who could not draw near of their own strength had themselves borne by others. 'Master, if you choose, you can cure me' were the words I heard. 'I do so choose; be cured.' would come as the reply.

In the confusion of these crowds I slipped away. I did this partly because of a boy's shame of his own emotions, partly because I was not anxious to embarrass the one who had been so good to me by clinging to his protection. But once more, going forth alone, I did so with a lighter heart than I had ever known before. Jesus of Capernaum had been a friend to me. If I never saw Him again, that friendship would still be the invigoration of my life. In the days that followed, among throngs which pressed about Him everywhere, I forced myself in scanning His beloved countenance and hanging on His words, though keeping myself unseen.

This I did while making the effort to bless those who cursed me, to treat those who ill-used me, well and to pray for those who abused me. Strangely, too, it seemed that in proportion as I tried to do this, those who had aforetime been cruel to me showed some sign of relenting.

Certain it is that I was neither robbed nor beaten quite so much. While those names as 'dog of a Gentile' were flung at me less frequently, when they were I sought opportunity to do kindness toward those who uttered them, often confounding their harshness, though sometimes receiving but blows in return. Nevertheless, I persisted, and when smitten did my best to pray for them who smote me.

This was the more difficult seeing that I knew no God. Of our Roman Gods I had so little that beyond such a name as Jupiter or Mars I had no learning. To the Jews', God I knew to be abhorrent. When, therefore, I put up my petition all I could think of was to lift my heart to the Father of Jesus of Capernaum - reasoning that the Father of such a Son would not say me, nay. I went before Him boldly, and do so to this day.

Of the Son, Himself, I lost no going nor coming, and no word. Wherever He was in public, there was I. Wherever He went, I tried to go too. Near the house in which He lodged was a garden of olives in which I could lie, and watch His door. If He came out, I followed Him, keeping out of sight, but with the distant vision of His person to encourage me. So it came about that I learned His ways, and often knew His errands before He set out on them. There servants and disciples whom I could question, and who seeing I loved Him, not seldom answered me.

To do something for Him who had done so much for me was that on which all my desire was set. For this I worked and saved money. Each day in a vineyard brought me in half a denarius. This I hoarded in an old leathern wallet I had found in the street of a town and now hung around my neck, inside my gabardine, for safety. Work being scarce, and my pay sometimes refused me after I had toiled for it, it was long before I had the three whole denarius I judged to be enough for the honoring of my Lord. Then on a day I learned that it was His purpose to journey next morning to Nazareth in the mountains where he had lived earlier. Further, He was to go alone, which would give me my opportunity.

For I had observed already that when He went alone He did not provide Himself with food. 'I have food to eat of which you do not know', was His explanation of this neglect of self. 'My food is doing the will of Him who has sent me and finishing His work'. But for me that was not enough. I had often seen that in places far from succor He was tired and hungry. Had I been able to minister to Him then it would have been my joy.

But here I found my occasion. As I lay in the garden near His house, watching before dawn, I saw Him come forth, turning His face towards the mountains. Immediately I hastened to the market which was opening for trade. There I purchased a basket in which I placed two wheaten loaves, the best that could be bought, a small round cheese no bigger than an apple which was a dainty of that country, a cake of dried raisins, and few figs.

My basket being lined with leaves of the vine, and covered with the same, the whole was protected. This care was the more needful since I should not see Him till the morrow, which would be the Jews' Sabbath. Then I knew that according to His custom He would go to their Synagogue, where His teaching might cause trouble.

Arrived at Nazareth, I found a cleft of a rock outside the town in a cool and secret place where I might hide my provender. Near it I passed the night to guard it from man and beast. In the morning I made my way to the Synagogue, finding myself in the general excitement, permitted to enter and sit down. A Jews' Synagogue is not like a Greek or Roman Temple, nor even like their own temple as I have seen it in Jerusalem.

It is but a plain rectangular room with benches. At one end is a platform where a president sits, behind him the scrolls of their law and prophets on shelves concealed by a curtain. Of priest or worship there is none. He who wills may stand up to read and address the assembly. He who wills may question the speaker, and where questions and answers are many there is frequently much discussion.

It being already noised abroad that He was in their town, every seat was taken. If anywhere there was room to stand, that place too was occupied. Some of the relatives were there, and many had known Him as a boy. From what I overheard, their attitude was unbelieving rather than inimical. They thought it a subject for laughter that one whom they had seen grow up in their town like any other lad should be among the prophets who were to redeem Israel.

'He may deceive Capernaum, Cana, Nain', I heard one say to another, 'Us He will not deceive. Have we not known His father and mother? Have we not known His brothers and sisters - they are here with us, Go to'. Thus with laughter on their lips and scorn in their hearts they gathered to see Him frustrated.

Presently He entered, calm, noble, head erect, the embodiment of strength and beauty. Making His way to one of the cross-seats parallel with the end of the platform, where all could see Him, and whence He would behold all, He sat down. For some reason beyond curiosity, as I afterwards came to understand, every eye was on Him. When the moment came He stood up, signifying that He would read from the book of their Prophet Isaiah. And this was the passage which He chose:

"The Spirit of the Lord is upon me, for He has consecrated me to preach the good news to the poor. He has sent me to announce to the prisoners their release, and to the blind their recovery of sight, to set the downtrodden at liberty, to proclaim the year of the Lord's favor.

On His handing back the scroll to the attendant there were some who murmured their applause. Others showed indignation that one whose father had been a carpenter of their own should assume such pretensions. Near where I sat a group of young men whispered and laughed behind their hands, not scrupling to make signs to one another, that if need arose, they would treat Him with violence. Seeing this I swore I would give my life before one of them should touch Him.

Nevertheless, like all others where ever He appeared, they watched to see Him work a miracle. Blind being there, and lame, and paralytic, they hoped He would heal as He had in the cities around about. Not only did He do nothing, but He told them why. Even in the Kingdom of Heaven, He said, the solitary worker's faith is not enough. It must have helpful cooperation. Where it is met by foregone distrust it is rendered ineffective. The Prophet is never without honor except among his own kin and his own country. It was to no widow in Israel that Elijah was sent, but to a woman of Serepta, a Sidonian. It was no Hebrew leper who was healed by Elisha, but Naeman, a Syrian....

Knowing in advance the conclusion to which He was leading them, they allowed Him to go no further. The point was one as to which Israel had always been sensitive, and never so much as then. The more this proud fanatic people lost their political independence the more tenaciously they clung to their spiritual eminence as the owners of the one true God. To say that even on occasions He should show to the Gentiles favors He did not extend to them was treason for which death was too light a punishment. Many of the Prophets had preached this doctrine and had been stoned for it. This pestilential fellow should be put out of the way by the easiest method known to them.

No sooner had they seized His point than the synagogue was in an uproar. Surging around Him they raged, denounced and threatened. But lifting their hands to strike Him, one was struck. There was that in Him, a majesty, a sacredness, which forbade the grosser forms of the insult. The worst they could do was by weight of numbers compel Him up their hill. Their city breaks to deep and dangerous precipice. 'To the rock!' were the cries about Him. The young men I had seen whispering in the synagogue made signs to one another how they would dash Him down. Men, women screamed at Him, children picked up handfuls of stones which they dared not throw. He, alone - superb and secure, was calm with the tranquility of strength.

Suddenly, with a gentle detaching movement of the hands, He put them all away from Him. There was no force in the action, beyond the force of command. But like children rebuked, they all fell back from Him. The old men ceased to curse; the younger ones to mock. Over the multitude silence fell, and strange amazement. He spoke not a Word, but, the way being free, He went on. From these eyes of memory the grandeur of that movement will never pass nor fade. Kings have I seen them, and Ceasars entering Roma in triumph after victory; but never one who carried with him the inborn authority of Jesus of Capernaum. Of Ceasar the imperial state was not in himself; but in his army, his trophies, his prisoners, his slaves, the adulation of citizens, many of whom hated him. This man was never so august as when alone before his enemies. Never angry, never resentful, never moved to avenge Himself by so much as a frown, His might of serenity must have moved the highest Gods, if such there be, to envy and imitation.

Of the Nazarenes all dropped from His path, while He went up to the brow of the cliff whence they would have hurled Him down. This He did without a companion and of His own free will. I, Galba, watched Him with the rest, but when they went back crestfallen to their homes, I crept thru bushes which hid me from sight and followed Him. Soon I perceived Him seated on a rock, gazing over the wide plain lying far below, called in the Jews' language Esraelon. His back being turned to me, I could slip away in search of my basket which concealed hard by, and with this in hand, I approached Him humbly.

Master, 'I faltered, be not angry. I have brought you food'.

In His face, as He looked toward me there was all the light and Love that could have blessed mankind.

Dear Boy', He smiled, 'have you followed me?'

Down on my knees before Him, I held out my basket as an offering. 'Only, Master, because I saw you were alone, and feared you might be hungry'.

'I am hungry', He admitted, 'Not having broken my fast since yesterday. Let us eat together'.

'Nay, Master', I pleaded, 'Lest there be not enough for two'.

Once more He shed on me the sunlight of His smile. 'In the Kingdom of Heaven there is always abundance. You shall see'.

'Master', I cried, 'where is this Kingdom? Is it far away? Could a Gentile boy ever enter it?'

As we ate, He explained the Kingdom, simply, and in words I could comprehend said that it was not far away, saying that it was not merely round about me, but <u>within</u> me. It was a way of understanding. It was seeing life and the world and all things as they are seen by God. God was the Great Father, the God Father, the Loving Father, the Source from which all our blessings proceed.

From this Source we receive not blessings and cursing together but only blessings; not sweet water and bitter, but only sweet. In that Kingdom, there are not evil things, no sin, sickness, poverty or unhappiness. For those whose minds are close enough to the Father of Life there is not even death. We are in this Kingdom when we know we are. Then having understood that fact, we create our own Heaven by admitting there nothing but the Rule of God.

With many other words, with parables and examples, He made this clear to me, till I think I seized it once for all. And before asking anything of myself, He told me something of His own boyhood in that very town of Nazareth, on the very spot on which we sat. He had been a boy like any other boy; He loved His games, His studies, His young friends.

But very early in His life, so early that He could not recall its beginning, His mind had been preoccupied with the thought that God was His Father; and if His Father, then the Father of every other boy, and if the Father of every other boy; then the Father of all men and women everywhere, then the difference between Jew and Gentile, Roman, Greek, Edomotte, broke down. Bond and free, rich and poor stood alike before God, the one as well as the other endowed with the right to spiritual grace and physical welfare.

Then it had come to Him the simplest way to test a conclusion was to act on it. That was all He had ever done, finding the reward so great that the people said He worked miracles. He had not worked miracles; He had only proved to Himself, and He hoped to some others, that the resources of the Kingdom of Heaven were infinite.

But it was where we sat that He had thought most of His problems out. Of His advances in understanding, each great feature of the landscape now stood like a monument. Calling my attention to the smiling beauty of the plain, He said that thus our life in the Kingdom of Heaven always seemed to Him.

The Valley of the Jordan, of which He could trace the line, with the rocky land of Persia on the other side, typified the harsh road along which our race had traveled to reach its present Knowledge of God, the long fringe of Carmel to the West, with its abrupt termination in the sea, marked the way to that wide Gentile world, over which He yearned and which meant the future of man's faith. Behind us to the South lay the gloomy mountains of Samaria, with the more sullen country of Judea, beyond them, the Altar of Sacrifice on which they would one day offer up the Lamb of God.

'And', quoth He, 'My work is not yet accomplished. I have still many truths to test, still new experiments to make. Even in the Kingdom of Heaven we progress as God gives us the ability. I have healed the sick, given sight to the blind, and released the sin-bound from their sin, but I have not yet raised the dead, nor showed that by His cooperation with the Father, any son of God can raise even when death has held him. Having conquered other things I must conquer death, and you, if you continue loving me, may see it."

So in sweet confidential talk the afternoon of that strange Sabbath passed, He never seemed to condescend to me, but to be a boy like myself. There was indeed something about Him of everlasting youth. It may have been His simplicity, or His innocence, or His love of the life out-of-doors, or the power to take things as they came, without regrets for the past or forebodings as to the future.

To the incident in the synagogue that morning He did not return, nor did it seem to sadden Him. All His discourse was as to pleasant things over which He often laughed right merrily. Because of His respect for the Jews' law of the Sabbath day's journey, we abode where we were that night, supping from the fragments in the basket. Strange to say these fragments provided us with plenty not only for the evening meal, but for the breakfast in the morning.

During the warm softness of the night He asked me of myself, learning the little I had to tell.

'Never forget', He bade me, 'that in my Father's house is your home. This means not a far-distant home which you can reach through the portal of death; but a home for your immediate use. If you have not found it hitherto, it is because you have not known how to seek it'.

'But, Lord, I have not known the right, nor do I now'.

Remember, the words I spoke only a few days since. Seek first the Kingdom of God, and uprightness before Him and all these other things: home, shelter, teaching, love, all that a little boy has need of, will be given you besides.

'But. Master, where shall anyone in Jewry give a home to a Gentile Boy?'

'In my Father's house are many mansions. Provisions are made for everyone. You will see; it will be a Gentile home, such as you are in need of. Now, that by loving and following me, you have so sought the Kingdom, its resources will be at your command'.

On the morrow as we descended toward Capernaum He told me of a Roman captain (Centurion) who was among His friends. Without having become a proselyte to the Jews' religion, as many did, this captain had loved the true and only God to whom the Jews' religion had introduced him. He became, too, a devout and earnest listener whenever the Master spoke.

"Now this man is beloved of his own slaves, whom he himself freely loves in return. It chanced that one day, not long ago, that one of his servants fell ill. On his appealing to me I answered that I would come and heal him. Immediately he said, 'I am not worthy to have you under my roof.

Speak the word only and my servant shall be healed'. Astonished at this, I told the multitude that I had not found anyone in Israel with so much faith. 'Go, I said to the captain. You will find it just as you believe'. 'This man, the Master continued, 'is still in Capernaum. He loves me; he is my friend. Whatever I ask him, he will do for me, and for you as well'.

Then I understood. With the Roman captain was to be my home, the Kingdom of Heaven would provide for me. But what would be a joy to me a few days earlier was now a grief.

'O, Master'; I cried, 'Why may I not follow you and be your servant?'

'Because, Dear Lad, the Father has work for you which could not be done in that way. You must grow up in the company of other lads. You must know the love and care of a family. You must learn and work and have a long life, with children and grandchildren to rise up and bless you. I have that to do in which no boy could share. Were you to attach yourself to me you would soon be alone again and insufficiently protected, but I shall not leave you; I shall not cease to bear you in my heart. If it be your will to continually love me, you will best show your love by living the life into which the Father will lead you'.

Thus it came to pass that I entered the Family of Publius Versus Lucillus becoming to him as a son. Not that he had no other sons. Three he had, and two daughters. Having been recommended by Jesus of Capernaum, I found myself welcomed by them all, clad and fed and taught like a Roman boy of better family than that from which I sprang. My one grief was that when the Roman power moved my foster Father from Capernaum to Tyre we went out of the sphere in which our Master worked. For nearly a year in Tyre little tidings of Him came to us and what we then received was worse than none at all.

Most of His time, he was spending now, or so we heard, in Jerusalem and the regions round about. There the Jews plotted to have Him slain. At last we were told that the approaching Passover would not go by without His being put to death a rebel against the Roman authority.

Then my foster father was sore distressed, and being on influential terms with Pontius Pilate, the governor of Jerusalem, he determined to travel hither and see what he could do by means of intercession.

As he was taking the slave who had been healed, I pleaded with him to also take me. This he did, for he treated me with love, and so with soldiers and servants we set out. Wherever we lay at night we made inquiries as to the fate of Jesus of Capernaum, but not until we reached Bethany, on the outskirts of Jerusalem, did we learn that He had been crucified on the previous day.

Of our mourning I will say nothing. Entering the city, my foster father sought Pilate, the Governor, whom he rebuked right bitterly. After that he stretched himself out on the earth, refusing food and comfort. Left to myself, I coursed the city, seeking of all and sundry such news of my Master's end as I could learn. Out to the Hill of Calvery I went, getting confirmation of the tales of the three empty crosses still standing on the place of Skull, as the skull-shaped summit of that hill was named. Nearby there was a garden where they told me He had been lain. A tomb, I found, beating my body against it, and shedding tears.

It being now near nightfall, I should have returned to the inn where our retinue lay, but to drag my footsteps from that Holy place was beyond my power. Accustomed to sleeping beneath the stars, I was unafraid, and food I could not have tasted. Some consolation it was to me to lie so near that beloved form, hidden out of sight though it lay behind a rock-hewn door.

The Jews' manner to bury differs somewhat from ours in that a chamber is hollowed in a rock which is often a solitary boulder. In this way a door is formed which slopes upward from the ground. This curving portal is so closely fitted that when shut it is one with the rock itself. Dashing myself against the hard rounded surface, I wore myself out weeping.

But by that time it was fully night, and the moon shining amid the glades of olive, cypress, and cedar, I had exhausted my tears and grown calm. All I could think of was that the adored form lay but two or three cubits away, within the impenetrable stone. Had I been permitted one last glance at the face and eyes which had never turned on me otherwise than in love, it seemed to me that my sorrow would have been lightened. But all was gone. Next day we would set out again for Tyre, and from there to Spain or Britain as the powers of Rome appointed. This incident would be over, and not so long as life lasted should I ever see my beloved Jesus of Capernaum again.

So, in silent sorrow, that night wore itself away. Next I slept not; I had no desire to sleep. All my consolation was to know that I was there, so near Him, though He had gone so far. I was seated in the grass, and yet so close to the tomb that at any moment I could touch it, while the Paschal moon bathed me round about.

This moon was soon to set. Where the open spaces of the garden had been bright they became blurred with darkness. The sycamores and cypresses which had stood out clearly against the purple sky now mingled themselves with it. I knew that dawn was not distant, though in the east there was as yet no sign of it.

For these reasons, a faint seam of light marking the line where the door of the sepulcher had been cut and refitted was the more visible. It was such a seam as will often be observed round a closed door in any dark chamber where a candle is burning on the other side. How long I had noticed it before becoming consciously aware of it, I cannot tell. Indeed, it seemed to me that it had been there throughout the night, that my heart had perceived it, though my eyes had been holden.

I was not startled. I had a little sense of the unusual. In my thoughts of Jesus of Capernaum there had always been so much of light that it did not seem strange that He should shed a brilliance (radiance) even in His grave. The one reflection I clearly recall was to the effect that if I later told anyone of what I was seeing they would not believe me. He would say that I was sleeping without knowing it. Wondering if that were not the case, I did the unusual things which people do to assure themselves that they were awake.

Some slivers and filings of stone left on the ground when the door had been drilled, I picked up and stowed in my wallet. These are the stones I have had incased in the golden shrine all my children will remember, I gathered them one by one so as to have something, if not much, to tell me that I was capable of action when witnessing wonders beyond any I have ever known in a dream.

I was still endeavoring to convince myself that I was awake when an even greater marvel came to my attention. For a space of perhaps the breadth of two fingers, the door of the sepulcher lowered itself gently. Remaining fixed for a few minutes, it closed again. Had I been on the top of the rock instead of at its base I could have peered within. A few minutes later this effect was repeated, the door standing open at the highest line for perhaps the width of a man's hand. While it did so the glow of light which streamed through the interstice was strong and unflickering, like that of no earthly candle. The action was noiseless, as if someone possessed of a kind of strength of which I had no knowledge was doing his best to roll back the slab from within.

On the fourth attempt the door remained open for at least two cubits, so that had I stood upright, I could have easily looked behind it. As it was, I lay prone upon the grass, amazed and excited, but too much overawed to forestall by a second that which might soon be revealed to me. But on this fourth attempt the open portal did not close again. Balanced on its base for a time, it finally powered itself, easily, soundlessly, till in the full width and length it fell beside me in the grass.

And there He lay, my Jesus of Capernaum, tall, straight, vigorously framed swathed in white, His features hidden by a gravecloth. Even to a boy I was then fourteen - the majesty of His Presence was heightened by the mystery and solitude of the grave. Here was that shrine of eternal loneliness, in which the busy crowded life of man works out to the peace of everlasting nothingness, as the body gives itself back to its primal dust.

Except for this disclosure to me, made with I knew not what intent, Jesus of Capernaum would lie there within the bosom of the rock while the ages rolled over Him, and till in the turmoil of new epochs His name would be blotted out. But there was a grandeur in that destiny, the spirit free at last of torment and futility, proof against pain forever.

As far as I found a reason for my being permitted to see what I saw, it was some kindly act of compensation for the denials which had shut me out from a share in the last days of the man I loved. I was to be allowed at least to view Him as He lay at rest. What great mystic power granted me this favor I could not guess, even the agency we call God being unknown to me except as the Father of Jesus of Capernaum. And great mystic powers were beyond my ken. Nevertheless, this boon had been granted, and so I lay prone, absorbing the details of the tomb in a manner to never forget them. Presently the great stone door would shut again and the line of light fade out in the common day.

Then - beneath the grave clothes, I saw a hand raised. It suddenly rose and fell. It rose and fell again. It was such a stirring within the cerements, sweet, faint, as you will sometimes see in the infant's frame before he awakes from sleep. Then for a long few minutes there was nothing, only the rigid outline, swathed in white.

I came to the conclusion that whatever the forces at work in this sepulcher, they could not be summoned at will. Force was somewhere striving with, force, the new overcoming the old, but only by the mightiest tests of strength. In the quiescent minutes I began to see a gathering of new energies, to result in further accomplishments.

Of these the next was the freeing of a hand. Bound as it was, it detached itself easily, gracefully, with no signs of struggle, but by means too quick for me to follow.

There was again a stillness, while the hand lay outstretched among the graveclothes, long slender, bronzed even the pallor, as I had so often seen it, but with a great healed wound in back and palm which might have been the mark of a wooden nail. That this wound should have healed so soon was in itself a matter of surprise. Nothing but awe held me back from seizing the hand and kissing it.

And presently it moved. It moved restlessly, aimlessly, till suddenly it brushed the face cloth from the face. This it did as if impelled by a power outside the mind's direction. The beloved features thus uncovered, were calm, and younger than I had remembered them. Quietly upturned, clearly cut, the crisp growth of beard, of the color of gold in which there is a strong alloy of copper, bearing its witness to His natural strength, they were the features of One whom the darker powers could never, as I see it now, have kept within their grasp. Needless to tell you I watched breathlessly.

And I watched long. So long it was that I now had seen His face, I began to think myself at the end of my strange privileges. It would soon be dawn and with dawn the sepulcher would close again, I should go my way to Tyre, to Rome, or wherever my future lot might be cast, but I should never forget that the Father of Jesus of Capernaum had allowed me this one look on the face of His dead son.

But as I was thinking this, there came a quiver of an eyelid. Later there was a twitching of the lips behind the beard.

Then the eyes opened. They opened like those of a newborn child. At first they seemed to see nothing, only to look. They looked ponderingly, wisely, as if judging of what they saw by other standards than ours. In color they were blue, but that of deepest sea blue, of richest sapphires, which is often almost black. For a time I feared that if they were turned on me He would no longer remember me.

But when they were so turned the action was again with a little child's lack of consciousness. At last there came a smile. It came slowly, but it never came so radiantly. Never, I think, could such a smile have been vouchsafed to any other creature in the world. 'Master; Master'; I cried, this time aloud, 'Dear little boy, 'was the response. 'Sweet it is to me to have you here'.

Beneath the coverings I could see the other hand seeking to free itself.

Master', I pleaded, 'may I not aid you?'

No, dear child. This is work which I must do alone. In conquering death I may use no help but the Father's. If I did, a large part of its meaning would vanish from my task.' 'But what is its meaning, Lord?'

The proving to my brethren that there is no death. Telling them would not be enough. I must show them the powers the Father has endowed us with, by using them. Even so, most of them will not believe me. They have seen me on the cross; looked on while I died; they watched while loving hands buried me. Nevertheless, few of them will accept the fact that I have risen even when they see me and talk to me as you are doing now.'

This, indeed, I could understand since I scarce accepted it myself. This man, I reasoned, could never have been dead, in any sense which I ascribe to death. His eyes shone, His lips smile, His voice rang with the freedom and force of living activity. How could He have been dead, when here He was so vitally alive.

Had I not actually gone through the change to which we have given the name death, I should not have been able to show on coming back that I have all the faculties of life. Soon you will see that I have more than you have hitherto known me to possess. This is much for my brethren to be assured of. They have been afraid of death. I myself shrank from it. That was because I understood it a little better than themselves. Now that I have been through it, and come back, I can show it as a fuller grasp of the Kingdom of God which here we seize but partially.

Suddenly He raised Himself, and sat upright. This He did with the grace of an athlete, all of whose muscles are as his command. Seated there He was as much at ease as if on a couch back in His chamber. The face cloth which had slipped to the rock floor of the sepulcher, He picked up and folded, laying it in a corner of the tomb, near the rough stone ledge, slightly hollowed out, which had served Him as a pillow. Concentrated as He was upon His purpose, He nevertheless continued speaking, gently, and in simple words, in order, apparently that I, a boy, should understand Him.

Were this great triumph of man over death to be wrought for my sake alone it would not have been worthwhile. Merely to magnify me would not be to help my brethren. The thing they must learn is that what I have done, they too can do. There is no need for them to pass through the horrors of pain and the grave in order to reach the next step in being; they can, at the appointed time, migrate of their own free will, as the birds fly north and south. My task is to show them that it can be done.'

But, Master,' I had the temerity to object, 'I see not how it can be done, even though I see you doing it.'

His smile was one of piercing sweetness. 'Dear boy, He said, not how it can be done, but that it can be done. That it can be done I can demonstrate to the eye. How it can be done is for each to discover for himself. Live simply and sinlessly; heal the sick; cast out the evils. He who does that will put off the life of time and put on that of the ages as a man casts aside an outworn cloak, and robes himself in one more glorious.'

But Lord', I murmured, 'will any man after you ever be equal to this thing?'

Not perhaps for a thousand years, as time is counted in the mortal world. Men in growing numbers will applaud the example I give them, but will make no attempt to follow it. That it implies sinlessness, or state as near to sinlessness as may be reached, will in itself keep men and women from awakening the powers which as yet are asleep in them, and will remain asleep for ages and ages to come. For ages and ages to come the seekers after truth will strive to find the way behind the veil by means of no great efficiency, advancing here, and losing ground there, but making little progress anywhere.

My way they will reject because it is too difficult, but by that time a new race of children of God will have been born. They will, they shall then return to what you; beloved lad, are witnessing this morning. They will see at last that once and for all the experiment has been made, and set themselves then to learn how. That how there will be then no reason to explain, since all but the vicious, will not only love God, but will understand Him.'

Even as He spoke, I began to see a change in Him. Hitherto He had been Jesus of Capernaum, such as I had known Him. Some slight difference there was, such as you will see in a man whom you have known in sickness when you see him well; but it was no more than that.

Now all at once He began to glow as if light was His raiment instead of such clothes as mortals wear or put on their dead. It was not on fire or flame or anything that burned; rather was it a self-illumination.

Nevertheless, He still continued to sit upright and speak to me, 'Above all things take heed to this, dear lad. It is not knowing about the Father that will prove to be Eternal Life; it is knowing Him. Understanding Him you will have in your hands a portion of His Power. You will be able to rule your life, freed from the tyranny of chance and circumstances. To me who have carried out the Father's will, all power is given in Heaven and Earth. To you will be given in like manner, according to the measure of your obedience.'

What happened next I saw not, even though I was looking on. It was action too quick and transcendent for my eyes to follow. He left the tomb. He was standing before me. Between the moment in which He sat addressing me and that in which He sat addressing or rather stood above me, my eyes on a level with His feet, there was not, as far as I could judge, the briefest interval of time. But there He was, moving as I had seen Him move in the past, only on feet of Light.

On feet of Light He was robed in Light; In the tomb the graveclothes lay empty and discarded. The face cloth was wrapped and apart, even as He had PLACED IT. Tall, erect, majestic, but loving and kind beyond all comprehension. He stood before me in raiment like unto sunbeams.

'Beloved boy,' quoth He, softly and strongly, you have followed me with a very sweet affection. Now I shall do the same with you. You will not see me, but I shall be there, helping you through a long mortal life that shall bring you both joy and care. Always remember that I shall never leave you nor forsake you.'

And then, as I knelt with my hands clasped looking up at Him adoringly, my eyes were unable to keep the vision. The beauty was too great; the radiance too intense. The inability was on my side. He grew too glorious.

In the garden it was dark, with the first of dawn in the darkness. There was no Light from the tomb, nor had I companionship. Moreover, two Roman guards who seemed to have lain nearby in drunken sleep awoke and began to curse. Unseen by them I slipped away.

Near the gate of the garden I passed three women, who were entering. I heard one say to the others, 'The spices we have brought, the ointments, and the linen; but who shall roll away for us the door of the sepulcher?' Hiding behind a sycamore I waited till they had gone by.

But when I told my foster father of how I had spent the night, and of what I had seen in doing it, he bade me to keep it secret, already he had heard whispers in the court of Pilatus that some trouble was afoot. The report had gone around that the body had been stolen while the soldiers slept and the governor feared a scandal. So, enjoining silence, and himself believing that Jesus of Capernaum was dead beyond resurrection, my foster father gave the word that we should set out that selfsame day for Tyre.

Ere long we were transferred from Tyre to Rome, to Colonia Agrippina on the River Rhine, from there to Londinium in the Province of Britannia. Here my foster father died and I grew to manhood, marrying a British wife. All my offices being in this distant portion of the Empire, I heard no more of Jesus of Capernaum till the other day. Then strange to relate, an old man, a wanderer, came to our town to deliver what he called an evangelium. His name was Joseph of the town of Arimatgea, in the Jews' country. All this way he had traveled, holding meetings in town after town, to deliver this message: that a man had risen from the dead. At once I sought him. 'Can it be, that He of whom you would tell us is one Jesus of Capernaum?' 'The same,' quoth he, 'Have you heard of Him?' 'Not only have I heard of Him', and 'Not only have I known Him, but in a garden in the Jews' City of Jerusalem, three days after His death, as the Jews reckon time, I saw Him as He.......'"

But here the Manuscript breaks off --

Note: All quotations from the NEW Testaments in the above, are taken from the American translation into modern speech, by Dr. Goodspeed.

Keep Thine Mind Staid on Me!

Mine Beloved Ones: Wherein hast thou been sufficient unto thine self? Wherein hast thine wisdom been sufficient? I ask of thee: know ye not that I am the Lord thy God - sent unto thee that ye might be staid in Me, and sustained by Me. I say unto thee thou art not alone, yet I say thou art alone in as much as thou art not sufficient unto thine self - for I say ye of thine own self can do nothing --- Yet through Me the Lord thy God - all things are possible. Yet I say, within thine self thou canst not accomplish that which shall be accomplished through and by Me.

Yet, too, I say: All the power, the credit, and the Glory unto the Father which hast sent me, and for this do I say unto thee, unto Him All the Glory and the praise, so shall ye remember Him first and last - and ye shall ask of Him thine freedom and give thanks unto Him. He is the One which hast sent Me and He is the cause of Mine being, hence unto Him goes the Glory and Praise. Yet it is written that "All things to their time and place." So shall it be, and I say that ye shall remember Me, and I shall find thee by <u>thine</u> <u>own</u> <u>light</u>, and for this have I said, let it so shine that I might see it.

From afar they shall come to seek thee out and to ask of Me, and I say unto thee there shall be ones which come asking foolish things. Some shall come seeking Wisdom, while others shall come and they shall be as the traitors. Yet I have said that <u>these</u> shall be exposed and <u>these</u> shall be cast out - and these shall be unto themself traitor; for I say they shall do no harm unto thee - yet ye shall be unto <u>them</u> no comfort. I say ye shall give unto <u>them</u> no comfort - for I say they shall not find comfort - they shall wait!

So be it that ye shall hold fast unto the law and be ye just in all thine dealings, and comply unto the law - and be ye circumspect in <u>all</u> thine ways and ye shall be unto thine own self true. Waste not of thine substance, waste not thine energy by spurious sayings - speak not as the foolish - for it is not becoming unto thee. I have said: "Keep thine Mind staid on Me" - Behold Me in Mine way - and walk ye in Mine footsteps and be ye learned of Me - and I shall lead thee out of darkness for this have I said: "Follow ye Me."

Now it is come when there shall be <u>action</u>; there shall be <u>great</u> <u>action</u>, and there shall be a separating - an accounting. The goats shall be separated from the sheep, and the goats shall be put into their places while the sheep shall be put into their places. Now I say I am not in the dark - I know one from the other. I know wherein they are, and I shall find them and bring them out --- this is that day! And it is the time of action and action there shall be - and it shall bring forth unity among Mine flock; for they shall be unified under one banner - the Cross and the Crown.

Yet I say ye shall not attempt to unify them by nor through thine efforts; for it is not so ordained; and it is not of man to be the organizer of these Mine Sheep. I say Mine sheep shall not be bound by any Earthly organization which holds them in bondage. They shall be freed from all bondage and they shall be as ones freed from all legirons. They shall have no bounds - they shall shake off their legirons and give unto Me their heart, their hand, their will as one single man - separate and apart, bound together only by and through the oneness of purpose, truth and justice, and this shall they "be". They shall be that which they profess - they shall live the law - and they shall bow unto no false Gods. They shall make for themself no idols. They shall pay no man a farthing for their freedom. They shall give no man a penny for his salvation. They shall seek of the Father and therein they shall find all which they need.

This is Mine Word unto thee this day - and I say unto thee, this is but the beginning; for I am now about Mine Father's business, and He hast entrusted me with this part. So be it I shall bring about Mine Strange Act, while they which do dream, dream still. I say I am here in the Earth as of flesh and bone, yet I am not bound by flesh, neither the law of Earth. I am a free born Man, born of Mine Father, I have won Mine Eternal Freedom. Never more shall I go into bondage, neither shall I know any limitation of any kind - for I Am the Lord thy God -

Sananda,

Son of God the Father, Solen Aum Solen -

Recorded by Sister Thedra

Qualifications of Character!

Beloved Ones: There are ones called out from among the unknowing ones, and the anti-Christs. While I say unto thee these which I have called out have been called for service in Mine Vineyard, and they have been given certain credentials which shall serve to identify them with Me --Yet I say unto thee the ones which I choose are the ones which have certain qualifications - such as stability of character - soberness of thought - sincerity of heart - and the mind to learn.

Yet I say unto thee: few have the Stability of Character to follow in Mine footsteps - few have the mind to follow Me --- Yet I say unto thee, it is now come when ye shall choose which way ye shall go - for there is little time in which to choose --- Yet I say for this do I speak unto thee that ye might know that the law is exacting and it faileth not.

While I have said ye shall choose which way ye shall go - I say unto thee: let it be the wise choice; for I say unto thee: the way of the transgressor is hard --- So be ye as ones true unto thine self and give not thine self the bitter cup. Rest not on thine laurels - and be ye not so foolish as to think thineself wise. So be it that I say unto thee, ye shall be as ones prepared for thine New part, and ye shall be as ones blest, for this have I given unto thee the laws. Yet I say unto thee: there are yet other laws to be revealed unto thee - and ye shall receive in the measure of thine preparation - so be it Selah.

Be ye as one blest of Me and by Me ---

I am the Lord thy God Sananda

Recorded by Sister Thedra

By What Hand Hast Thou Been Spared?

Beloved ones: wherein hast thou been staid? - Wherein hast thou been kept? - I ask thee wherein hast thou been kept? - By what hand hast thou been spared? - By what love hast thou been sustained? In whose time hast thou been sent forth? - And by which hast thou walked? I ask of thee by whose wisdom hast thou come into Being? On what hast thou relied, and on what hast thou lived? Wherein hast thou been sufficient unto thine own self?

Now, while I do remind thee of these things, I say unto thee thou hast not remembered Me, neither hast thou had thine Memory returned unto thee; and I say unto thee ye shall be as ones prepared to receive it. Yet why dost thou rebel against Me, that which I give unto thee? I say I am He which hast brought thee hence, and I am He which hast sustained thee. I am He which hast brought thee hence! And I have provided for thee. I have given unto thee of Mine Self, and I am not to be denied--for without Me thou should not be---

Now while I say I have provided for thee--I say unto thee I have brought thee forth--I have given unto thee that which thou callest

"Mind" - and I sent thee out pure - unadulterated. Thou wandered long in the lands of other realms - other planes. Other palaces hast thou occupied, and other lands hast thou occupied. Thou hast peopled Principalities and Cities. Thou hast brought forth fruit of great renown. Thou hast been both pauper and King. Thou hast sung great paens of praise unto the Lord of Hosts--- Yet this day I find thee as ones stumbling in darkness, crying for light, knowing not which way to go.

I say unto thee cry no more--be ye as ones prepared to return unto thine rightful Estate--be ye as ones thoughtful of Me, and give unto Me credit for being thine Father. Ask nought of them bound. Yet I say unto thee I have sent unto thee ones which shall assist thee, and these thou shall assist--these thou shall remember--these ye shall respect--these ye shall give unto as thou would unto Me; for these are Mine--these are Mine hands, Mine feet.

While they are not the fullness of Me, they are Mine hands, Mine feet. They serve Me within thine realm, and ye shall not spit upon Mine foot--and ye shall not despise Mine hand, neither Mine Word; for by Mine word hast thou been sustained, and by Mine word shall ye be brought home--and for this shall I send Mine Son unto thee and He shall prepare thee for to enter into Mine place of Abode. Loiter not in the darkness.

Yet I say ye shall comply with the law which hast been given unto thee - for Holy is the word, and great the power thereof. Mighty is the hand of Mine Son--and Mine Words shall He manifest before thee. Be ye as one blest of Him and by Him.

I Am thine Eternal Father

Solen Aum Solen

Recorded by Sister Thedra

Mine Mercy is Unbounding!

Mine Beloved Ones: Thine hands hast been filled by Mine Grace - thine eyes hast not yet seen the Glory of Mine storehouse - Mine Mercy is unbounding; and I say unto thee thine hands hast been filled by Mine Grace, and Mine Mercy I have extended---And I am the One which hast held thee fast in the times of thine rebellion---And too I say unto thee Mine Word is sufficient unto the day. I say I have given unto thee abundantly and I have given unto thee that which should satisfy thee--yet thou hast not known that which I have said. While I have been unto thee Merciful, thou hast rebelled against Me.

Now I say unto thee prosper thine self - be ye as ones justified, and be ye as ones worthy of all thine blessings which so generously come unto thee by Mine Grace. While I say thine blessings by "Mine Grace", I say that there are ones which I have sent that thine own wants be supplied that the way be made clear before thee--for this hast Mine Host come into thine realm that there be light. Now I say let the light so shine that ye might be prepared to return unto Me with the Lord of Hosts, I say with Mine Son which I have sent.

While I have sent Him that ye might be delivered out--I say ye shall be prepared for to receive Him for by thine light shall He find thee--by thine own light shall He find thee. And I say unto thee none other shall carry thee upon his shoulders - for thou art responsible for thine own self. Let none be unto thee a tack in thine shoe. Arise and come home- be ye as one returned unto Me. While I say unto thee Arise! Come home! I say unto thee thine strength - thine own effort - thine WISDOM is <u>NOT</u> sufficient unto thine deliverance--for this have I sent Mine Son- for He is the door through which ye shall enter into the place of Mine Abode - So be it Selah---

Mine time hast come, and I shall be as one which hast waited thine return. Now I bid thee make haste - receive Mine Son unto thine self and He shall give unto thee that which shall suffice thee. Mighty is the word and great the power thereof - and He shall speak the Word - and it shall set thee free, so let it be.

I am the Father from which thou hast gone forth--I am thine Father Eternal -

Solen Aum Solen.

Recorded by Sister Thedra

West Coast Land Shift

Beloved ones the time is come when there shall be great manifestations and great power shall be released upon the Earth-- and great energy shall be released from within the Earth-- and there shall be the first of a series of shocks which shall disturb the land and the waters of the coast wherein thou art,* and I say unto thee the waters shall roll and seethe and the land shall rise and fall and it shall quiver and surge--

I say it shall be as nothing which thou hast seen!

And for the time I say unto thee make no change which would take them into the place wherein there is great danger-- for therein is wisdom-- I say unto thee make no changes in thine residence for the time being-- for I say unto thee there is great danger within the coastal places-- while I say unto thee there is great danger I shall not alarm them for they have been warned and they have not heard neither are they prepared-- now I say it is come when great energy shall be released which shall raise the waters and lower the land, it shall lower the waters and raise the land-- so be it that I many shall be caught within the change and shift of land and water and they shall cry out for help in their panic-- I say unto thee they shall cry out in their panic--yet I say they shall be trapt-- they have been warned—

AND THEY HAVE NOT HEEDED MINE WORD----

I speak unto thee for thy own sake-- and I say it is not a far off when they shall cry unto thee for help-- So let it be for the good of all that I have spoken.

I SAY UNTO THEE FOR THE GOOD OF ALL I HAVE SPOKEN---

I Am the Lord thy God

Sananda, .Son of God

Solen Aum Solen

* Mt. Shasta (Pacific Coast)

Recorded by Thedra

Sign of Judgement

Beloved Ones -- While I say unto thee - prepare <u>thyself</u> - I say unto the <u>sleepers</u> - prepare! - Prepare! - for the day of awakening is nigh -- And too I say - many shall go into their next place of abode unprepared -- While it is yet time - I cry unto them - prepare thine self for thine new place -- Let it be for the better -- While I stand and call unto them - they sleep on -- I have said - "The sleepers sleep yet"-- So be it that they shall have another day in yet another place -- Yet I say - awaken! - Awaken! - be up and about thine Fathers business - while it is yet time for therein is wisdom - and therein ye shall find mercy -- I have said it is merciful to warn them - yet they accept it not ---

I say: When they do turn from their own willful ways - and seek the Light which I AM - with their whole heart - they shall find it -- For this have I come -- Now I say unto thee - ye shall remind them of these Mine Words - and they shall be as ones responsible for that which they do with them -- So be it that they which doth take heed of Mine Words, I say these shall I remember in the days of stress ---

Be ye as Mine hand made manifest unto them - and pray for the unknowing ones - that they might find mercy -- For I say unto thee - I have extended Mine hand -- They have but to accept it in Mine Name, For I AM the Lord thy God --

Sananda - Son of God

Recorded by Sister Thedra

Ref:-The prophesies of disaster (West Coast Land Shift) which has been given previously - to the Calif storms and earthquakes - tornadoes and other Earth disturbance ---Thedra

Great Stress Shall Come Upon All People

Mine Children: This day I say unto thee: be ye as ones prepared for thine new part- for it is now come that great stress shall come upon the peoples of the land-- and they shall not know peace- they shall cry "PEACE" and there shall be NO peace-- for I say unto thee: they have betrayed themself, and their trust.

I say unto thee: THEY HAVE BETRAYED THEMSELF AND THEIR TRUST! Now they shall cry out for mercy and there shall be no Mercy for the unjust.

I say Justice is Justice and shall reign supreme-- and justice is no respector of person-- for I say unto thee- justice is the exactment of the law- and no man takes from or adds to; for the law is not changed by man-- and his will changes it not!

While I say unto thee: the traitors shall find no Mercy-- I say too- that the just shall be dealt with justly; and they shall too find Mercy - and these shall I deliver out- for these are the ones which shall keep mine commandments- obey Mine word- and give unto Me credit for being that which I AM-- and unto these shall I say, PEACE; and unto these shall I show Mercy- For I AM Merciful-- I AM thine Father Eternal, Solen Aum Solen which hast given unto thee life, and wherein thou art staid.

Now I say unto thee: hear ye Me and remember well that which I say unto thee for ye shall have reason to remember it.

Solen Aum Solen Hast spoken from out the Center of Creation and thou hast heard Me, Mîne child- be ye blest of Me and by me, so shall it ever be. I AM thine Eternal Father----

Recorded by Thedra

THAT WHICH I AM

Behold Mine hand -- I say unto thee - behold Mine hand -- See it move, For I say unto thee - I Am the Lord thy God - sent of Mine Eternal Father that there be Light in the Earth -- And I AM that which I AM - and no man shall be unto Me the "tack in Mine shoe" for I shall have no other Father - for I Am born of Mine Father - the <u>First Cause</u> -- Supreme is He - and none other shall be unto Me Greater - for unto Him all the credit - all the Glory -- For HE is the Eternal Father of ALL that is Eternal - that which shall endure throughout the eons of time -- For He is TRUTH of the First Magnitude - and HE hast ALL POWER ALL WISDOM - and unto Him - all the Glory -- Look not to man for thine sustenance -- Look not for glory -- Look not for recognition -- For I say - men do but sit in the dark places and prattle* - and barter - and they know not the Eternal Verities -- They boast of their wisdom and power - yet I say they shall stand powerless before the elements - which would be unto them their handmaidens - were they so wise -- I say - were they "wise"- they would be unto themself sufficient -- They would have the power to control the elements - and they would know the law They would separate the sheep from the goats -- Yet they know them not apart - I say - I have sent Mine Servants into their midst - and they know them not -- They have not heard <u>them</u> - yet they expect Me - while they reject Mine Servants -- I say unto them: ye unholy wretches!

Why art thou so foolish? -- I say unto thee - <u>Why art thou so foolish</u>?

I say unto them - first ye receive Mine Servants in Mine Name -- <u>Then</u> I shall make Mineself known unto thee -- For how canst thou love Me - if thou hatest thine brother - which thou hast with thee - which thou doth see? ---

Be ye as one prepared to receive Me - and of Me -- Love ye one another -- I have spoken unto them which have ears to hear - and a mind to comprehend -- So shall I speak again and again --

I AM HE Which IS - and EVER SHALL BE -

The Son of God the Father -

The Lord thy God

Sananda

Recorded by Sister Thedra

* - To the ones who think they have it all -- T-

Such is Mine Great Joy

By Mine own hand shall ye be unbound and I the Lord thy God shall bless thee by the spoken word. And by Mine own mouth shall I speak the word which shall unbind thee- for this do I say unto thee be ye as one prepared to receive Me and of Me the Lord thy God- which cometh unto thee through and by the grace of Mine Father which hast sent Me unto thee-- Such is Mine great joy-- for this do I say be ye blest of Me- for I shall bless thee as thou hast not been blest---

So be it that ye shall receive of Me as I have received of Mine Father Solen Aum Solen. While I say unto thee He hast sent Me- I say I come by His grace and through His mercy- And I am glad-- Now I say unto thee praise ye the Name of Solen Aum Solen- for he is the Father of All of us which hath eternal life- and sing ye the paeans of praise for unto Him all the <u>praise</u> and the glory- forever and forever--- So be it, Selah. I am not as yet come unto the world of men- yet I say unto thee I have revealed Mine self unto thee that ye might be prepared to give unto them that which I give unto thee for them.

Yet I say as they are prepared so shall I give unto them that they might be prepared to receive Me and of Me-- And when it is come that I make Mine grand appearance I shall know them for have I not written upon their forehead their Name, their New Name?

And these shall know Me by Mine New Name and these shall be gathered up and they shall be part of the host which I bring with Me- So be it-- I have come as a thief in the night and found them sleeping-- too, I say that they shall awaken when the day comes wherein they shall be taken-- therein they shall await another day-- all which doth reject Me shall be put into a new place wherein they shall wait. I say their waiting shall be long and hard.

Yet, it is the law by which they are judged-- I do not sit in judgment- for I am not the Judge--- I am the Lord thy God. I bring the law and I say unto thee I point the way. Ye have but to walk therein- for I say none shall walk therein for thee---

Ye shall choose which way ye go---So be it thine own responsibility-- for I say unto thee I am not responsible for thine waywardness-- I am not responsible for thine salvation. I am only responsible for Mine own part-- for this do I say unto thee prepare thine own self- for the time draweth nigh when ye shall account for thine own Self. And ye shall be dealt with justly, for justice shall prevail-- it is the law of justice which I bring unto thee. So be it. Selah--- Now give unto them this Mine Word and let it suffice that I am the Lord thy God- Sananda, Son of the Most high living God--- the Father Eternal---

Solen Aum Solen

Recorded by Thedra

Mine Chosen Ones

Beloved ones- Mine day is come when I come into the world of man and wherein I shall take up Mine abode until I have found every one of Mine chosen ones- and they are now being called forth- and they are beginning to stir for they are now for the first time beginning to see part of the great plan- and I say unto them arise! Come forth- and be ye made whole for I Am the Lord thy God- and I say unto thee: Ye shall be as one prepared for to receive Me and that which I have for thee- for I say unto thee I have kept thine inheritance which is a princely inheritance- and it is given unto Me to know- for I have received Mine.

So be it that I have Sibored thee well- and I say unto thee ye shall arise upon the dawn as ones alert- as ones prepared for the new day which begins in the East- and ends in the East- I say unto thee there is no end unto the Eternal day, and ye shall walk straight ahead, and look not backwards- for to do so is the greatest of folly- Wheat shall grow the seeds of wheat- and thorns shall grow on thorn bushes- and Mine chosen shall do Mine works- which I give unto them to do- call not the chaff wheat- neither call the wheat chaff- and be not caught up in the thorn bush- for they but tear thine flesh- be ye as ones free to do Mine bidding- and harken unto Mine voice- and do ye Mine bidding-- and I shall lead thee into the place of Mine abode wherein there is no darkness- such is Mine word unto thee- and no man shall make void Mine word for I Am the Lord thy God-- sent of Mine Father that ye might be free from all darkness forever-- be ye as ones prepared to receive Me and of Me- for I cometh as a thief in the night when none expect Me- yet I say I shall reveal Mineself unto them which keepeth watch- and believeth upon Me- and I say unto thee be ye not part of their unbelief- for I Am with thee-

I Am Sananda- Son of God the Father- Solen Aum Solen

A Time of Maturing

Beloved ones: There is a time for growing to <u>MATURITY</u>- and there is a time of aging- and the aging is rather a time of Maturing-- the coming of age- when one becomes accountable of all that they do- and say-- when they have within their hand the power of direction through- and by the force of light Which I Am- I say when they reach the age of accountability they are within themself sufficient for they know themself and that which they are- they have the love of God within them-- they know themself to be one with Him and they are at peace and poise-- for this is the time when it is given unto them to grow into maturity wherein they know themself to <u>BE</u> Sons of God the Father Solen Aum Solen---.

I say unto thee ye shall see the foolishness of their childishness- and their own willful way- yet I say ye shall bear with them for a time and it shall pass with the maturing- I say they shall mature in due season: Now ye shall be as one prepared for the greater part-- while I say the lesser part hast been given for a preparation for the greater- I say ye shall give not thineself over to frivolity for it is but the foolishness of the little ones-- be ye as Mine plowmen- and break the soil for Mine words- sow ye the seed which shall grow and mature in a mighty harvest- So be it that I shall follow thee- and I shall gather in the harvest- and it shall be great indeed- for I say unto thee it is now come when ye shall see the results of thine labors which thou hast done in the time past which hast not been in vain-- So be it that ye shall find thine reward great indeed- So be it as thou hast prepared thine self so shall ye become - I Am with thee- I AM the Lord thy God- Sananda

Recorded by Thedra

I Shall Not Forget

Blest art they which cometh unto this altar-- for I say unto thee they shall be remembered in the time which is to come-- I say they shall be remembered for their coming and they shall be glad for the remembering--- So shall it be that they shall give heed unto that which is said unto them and they shall be as ones prepared to receive Me.

Now I say unto thee: these which I bring unto this altar shall have a part in Mine house-- and they shall be as ones prepared for that part which I have for them-- for it is given unto Me to know that which they are prepared to do. And not all are awakened- some are as yet asleep- and they slumber in the places of darkness-- yet I say unto thee: the call is gone out- and it has been given unto me to see them stir- yet they are not all awakened from their slumbers-- while I say unto thee: they shall awaken and arise and come forth as Lazarus from the tomb.

I say the veil shall be torn away- and they shall sleep no more-- for this do I say: ARISE! COME FORTH! AND BE AS ONES PREPARED TO FOLLOW ME!

Unto thee, I say follow ye where I lead thee and thine VICTORY is assured thee. So be it I have spoken and I shall not forget that which I have said. So be it and SELAH.

I AM the Lord thy God Sananda, Son of the Father Solen Aum Solen.

Mine Fold is Three-Fold

Beloved: It is given unto Me to see the signs of the time and I say unto thee: It is now the time to bring forth from out the world of men Mine disciples which have waited their calling.

I say unto thee: Mine chosen have waited for this day when they should be prepared for the call- and I say it is given unto Me to know where to find them.

Let it be said that we of the higher realms have waited too- for the time wherein they might be in embodiment upon the Earth and prepared for <u>this time-</u> now wherein do I find them? I say I find them sleeping in strange folds- for they are as yet not awakened unto their own identity.

Now let it be said that I have other folds which they know not of- yet they shall come to know that which ye know-- Mine fold is <u>Three Fold</u>- and I say they shall come to understand the meaning of this word* which I give unto thee-- for it is not a strange tongue that I speak-- I speak not foolish sayings-- I say unto thee I am a sober man and I am not given unto frivolity or foolishness-- I am the Lord thy God- sent that there be light among Mine PEOPLE-- yet I say unto thee- some are as yet asleep. They have as yet not awakened unto their own Identity-- yet they shall-- for I say I shall cause them to awaken and they shall ARISE and come forth from their slumbers- so be it that I say unto them: SLEEP NO MORE for it is now time to ARISE-- come forth as Sons of God -- so be it I am come that they might ARISE.

I AM Sananda Son of God the Father Solen Aum Solen.

* "This word"-- the scripts- which He hast given here.

Recorded by Thedra

Thanksgiving

Beloved Ones:

I speak unto thee as a mighty voice from out the Temple of the MOST HIGH LIVING GOD. I say unto thee; be ye as ones forever with me--for this do I speak unto thee as one sent of the great Father which is the Creator, which is everlasting- and real-pure and perfect.

I say unto thee, PRAISE HIS HOLY NAME! Shout it from thine heart let it ring forth in thanksgiving of His mercy--let it ring unto all the lands--and let it be heard by all men everywhere! For such praise shall be picked up as a glad anthem and as a paean of praise--and no man can swell it, neither detract from it for I say the praise of thine heart shall go out unto all the lands as a paean of thine own, and it shall be heard!

And the multitudes shall join in the paean of praise--let it go forth this day that all might catch the fragrance thereof- that all might know the joy of thine own heart- let it ring out! Let it swell upon the ether, let it fall upon their ears that they might know the joy of thine heart- let thine own gladness be multiplied to the greatness of HIS joy- to the magnitude of HIS joy when one has returned unto HIM, for there is no greater joy within the Fathers realm.

I say unto thee let thine heart rejoice this day, that "THIS DAY" is come--PRAISE YE HIS HOLY NAME-give thanks in all things for He is mighty and strong! He is merciful and loving--for this hast He said: "COME HOME MINE CHILDREN, COME HOME."

For this do I now say unto thee: "REJOICE!" that it is now come that ye shall return unto HIM. From out the Cosmos have I spoken-- from out the silence have I spoken, and I say unto thee: I am one which ye shall come to know. So be it Selah.

I AM he which ye shall come to know,

Recorded by Sister Thedra

Father Mother God and Son

We come in silent meditation--wordless we come, for no words of ours are necessary in this "HOLY COMMUNION". Let us partake of the 'BODY OF CHRIST' with great joy and thanksgiving--we offer ourself as a living sacrifice at this thine altar--unto the "MANY MEMBERED BODY" of Christ, that we might eat of the Bread of TRUTH which sustains us--let us drink freely of the wine of Spirit, which quickens and refreshes us- which makes us one with Him in this 'many membered body' which is Christ, the "ROCK" upon which this Temple is founded. We ask of thee Father, let it be according to thy will.

Beleis, so may it be.

It Shall Not Be unto Them Freedom

Be ye as Mine hand and give unto them this word- for I say unto them this day- as of old- the time is now come when the Son of God walks in their midst and they know it not- they have not the will to seek Me out- they are as ones burdened and sick of heart yet they look in strange places for their salvation. While I say unto them look unto the source of thine being for salvation- they give credit unto their fellow men which are bound by their own wanton and blindness- I say the world of men hast not found their salvation in the "World of Men" for they are but the creators of all that which hast tormented them-

I say they have not been freed by or through their sciences, their knowledge of machinery - yet they create greater and more complicated machinery that they might be free from the gravity of the Earth- yet they shall be tormented in their efforts- I say they shall be tormented in their efforts: for it shall not be unto them freedom! for they shall still be bound by the attraction of the Moon- and all their efforts shall be in vain- So be it that I am come that they be free from all bondage whatsoever!

I speak as one which knows wherein their freedom lies- So be it I am one free- therefore I know whereof I speak-

Now I say unto thee: give unto them this word and add unto it this:

I AM The Wayshower, come that they might be brought out of bondage- and there are none which are bound which have come into the place wherein I am, for they are free. While many free born men walk within the shadow, ye have not recognized them as yet- for they are gentle- they are quiet- they walk softly, unknown, unsung- and as for that unheard- they are the "Silent helpers" they are the balance force which have been established upon the Orb Earth that it might be spared the fate of the one known as Carr, which the forces of darkness once destroyed-

Now I say unto them: 'the forces of darkness' that they shall not destroy the planet Earth, for at the opportune time they shall be instantly removed! In the twinkling of an eye shall it be; and they shall be no more loosed upon the Earth, for I see the end of their activity, and they shall end! For this are these silent guardians sent that it be ended-

I say the end is in sight- so be ye at peace Mine beloved ones! Be ye still and know that I am the Lord thy God--.

Sananda

Recorded by Sister Thedra-

Establish Peace

Sanat Kumara

Sori Sori- Beloved of Mine being, I speak unto thee this day of peace- Peace which is Peace- Permanent Peace would I give unto them which know not such Peace- While it is given unto Me to know peace which is established within Mine own being- they know not of it- neither do they accept which I have offered unto them--.

Now it is come when they shall cry out for such as I have for them- they shall call out in their suffering and misery for they shall be sorely oppressed- while it is given unto them to be bound in darkness, I say unto them awaken! Be ye as ones come alive and arise out of thine lethargy and follow where the Lord thy God points thee- He is the way, the life, the light and He hast provided a place for thee- and yet thou hast rebelled against Him- thou hast not accepted that which He hast said unto thee- thou hast not <u>heard</u> that which He hast said for thou hast not opened up thine hearts for Him to enter in- I speak unto them which <u>think</u> themself sufficient- think themself wise- be ye as ones which have put off the old and turn thine face homeward- and ask of the Father, thine source for comprehension- while it is thine source of being it shall be thine own responsibility to establish peace within thine own self- be ye not disturbed for their wanton ways- their aggression- their "Sins" for it is the will of the Father that "YE" be at PEACE-.

While it is said: "The winds shall blow, the tempest rage- no harm shall come nigh unto thee so long as thou art at peace, peace, peace, I would have thee establish within thine own self-

So let it be-

I Am

Sanat Kumara

Recorded by Sister Thedra

The Law is Explicit

Pardon unto all them which revileth against Me- yet I say unto them! be ye as ones responsible for thine reviling for I the Lord shall raise Mine hand against thee and I shall cut thee off from the way which I have gone- for I say there are none which enter into Mine place of abode unprepared- for this do I give unto thee the law- I ask naught save obedience unto the law- I say none come into the place wherein I am unprepared- for this do I give unto thee the key- the law is explicit and it shall be exacting- bear ye thine own responsibility and falter not for it is nigh the end-

Be ye as ones come alive and hear ye that which I say unto thee, forget not that I am the Lord thy God and I stand as one prepared to deliver thee up- yet I say it is thine own choice- follow where I lead thee, Oh MAN of EARTH! Hear ye Mine cry! I bid thee return unto Mine Father with Me- for I come that ye be brought out of darkness: for this have I foresworn Mine home in glory that I might come into the world of man as one of thee- that I might touch thee with Mine own light- that I might put Mine foot upon the soil of Earth- that I might charge it with Mine life stream, Mine light, Mine own radiance which is His, the Fathers-

Yet beloved ones, Mine light diminished when I placed Mine foot upon the Earth for none could endure such a charge as I bring or as I brought- for none- NO NOT ONE! was prepared to receive in so great a measure- for did I not lower Mine light for their sake?

Now it is said: "NEVER AGAIN SHALL I LOWER MINE LIGHT FOR THEIR SAKE"

I say, ARISE! Ye children of Earth and come forth- follow ye Me that where I go ye might go also-

So let it be as ye will it--.

I Am the Lord thy God

Sananda

Recorded by Sister Thedra

O, Father!

O, great and glorious Father Mother God hast thine hand not been merciful unto us in our times of trial- hast thine love not preserved in this day? O, precious is thine love, thine name I would utter in hushed tones- for Mine love knows no bounds, it is by thine grace and love, thine compassion that thou hast sent Me unto these thine children for which thou hast so tenderly cared-

I bless them Father as thou would have Me bless them-.

Thou knowest the meditations of their heart - O, Father, cause them to awaken unto the fullness of thine love and mercy-

So be it I speak unto thee that they might hear Me- for thou knowest that which I Am- that which I say and do-

It is for their sake that I speak unto thee thusly for art We not one O, Father? I have spoken unto thee of them-

Now I speak unto them: Now ye Mine own beloved children hear ye that which I have said unto Mine Father, on thine behalf do I speak, for I have returned unto Mine Father and all is well with Me--.

So let it be with thee- for this have I said follow ye Me--

I AM Sananda

Recorded by Sister Thedra

The Great Wrath

Be ye as Mine hand and give unto them this WORD- and MARK it WELL!

I say unto them which have called themself "Christians" they have been unto Me a <u>stench</u>- and a blot upon society! I say they have been satisfied to sit in their high places which they appoint unto themself and they appoint their servants lesser stations- and they give unto themself titles which distinguish them above the servants- and they classify them according to rank and they give unto them power to oppress the "lesser brother" they give unto them power and authority to go into their private places and take from them their sons and send them into war- one against the other- and they give unto them shining medals of honor for service rendered- they dine and wine them: with song and music they stir them into action and call it patriotism and with no thought of the Christ do they these things- Yet I say they dare make a mockery of the name- they have been long at this unholy practice -.

Now I say the day of decision is come when they shall be dealt with-- when they shall see the folly of their practices- .

Now let it be said here- this day that the <u>CHRISTIANS</u> are ones which obey the law of love one for the other, they go not into battle! for I say they are <u>obedient</u> unto the law- they are as brothers- they fear NOT! They <u>know</u> wherein they are staid, they are as the gentle ones- they need no weapons - they are armed with the armor of God! they are as ones prepared to go all the way with a brother- they know all men to be brothers- while I Say: "they know all men to be brothers" I say there are those which are soulless- and these come to divide and destroy- for they are of the dragon sent- <u>many</u> serve him the dragon, unknowingly- unwillingly, yet I speak unto them fearlessly and frankly that they might know the true from the false-

I say all is NOT well within thine world which man hast fashioned!! Let thine eyes be made to see- thine ears to hear- and thine mind to comprehend the truth- for it is but the way of the dragon to deceive thee-

I say the Christian goes not into war- battle one with the others- neither against principalities- for he has his feet shod with light and his head is covered with the dawn of light- his heart is pure, and he knows wherein he is staid- he grovels not for pittance- he boasts not of his patriotism- his accomplishments- his conquests, his victories- He shares that which he has and asks nothing in return for he knows that his needs are known unto the Father which is his source- so be it that I am the Lord thy God--

And I say unto thee--

I am not of a mind to satisfy their selfish longings or give of Mine energy that they be satisfied!

I say they shall be brought to account for their foolishness and their vain glory shall be as the great wrath which they have set into motion.

So be it I have raised Mine voice, and I am not finished--.

I Am Sananda

Son of God-

Sent that there be light- so shall there be and great shall be the power thereof--

I AM and I know that which I AM

Recorded by Thedra

The Stepping Up

This day let it be established that there are many spheres, many orbs, many planes, many places throughout the solar systems- systems beyond thine system- systems to numerous to count- each bearing life-

life more glorious than thou hast known upon thine orb of Earth- yet Mine beloved ones- it is given unto Me to know these of which I speak- I say I know systems without number- to numerous to count and these are of the Fathers creation, He hast given unto Mine keeping the planet Venus and for that matter I have adopted the little star called Earth- for wast it not said that I came unto her when she wast in dire distress- It is so- so shall I always hold her dear unto Mine heart- and I shall not forsake her now--

While it is given unto Me to be the Lord of Venus, I say unto thee Mine beloved brother Sananda hast chosen to come into this Solar System as the Lord God of this system- I tell thee He is the Lord God of the solar system and He hast as yet not finished His work therein- for He hast but a short while ere it is finished - then He shall go on unto yet other worlds- other systems which ye know not of- for this is He now preparing Himself- and there are ones being groomed to take His office of Lord God- for He shall have yet another- another beyond His present station--

While I say others are being groomed for His office- that which He now holds, I say thou too art being prepared for greater places, parts. Waste not thine energy- for it is now come when great things shall be demanded of thee: and ye shall be as ones called upon for that which shall be given unto thee to do-- which shall be for the good of the whole- while I say unto thee thou as yet knoweth not the great work which hast been accomplished while thou hast walked blindly--

I say thou hast not been aware of the great things which hast been accomplished by thine work, through thine efforts- so be ye as ones blest, and be ye alert for I am come that it be So--.

I Am thine older brother and thine Sibor

Sanat Kumara

Recorded by Thedra

The Glory of God

While it is as yet not known unto thee the magnificent grandure of the glory of the Lord- I say unto thee, the glory of the Lord surpasses all thine imagination for no man hast imaged such glory-.

For thine eyes hast not beheld such glory! Thine eyes could not look upon such glory, such beauty, such radiance without He lowered His light--

So be it that this is the last time that this be done- I say no more shall the light be dimmed or lowered by taking up mortal flesh- for this have I said it shall be finished - done with- for never again* shall it be dimmed- lowered by Earth Vibrations- the vibrations of Earth shall be raised, and its people raised up- and none which are of darkness shall prevail against them, the forces of light, for this is the time of the end- when it is come upon the Earth that which was told of old- when there shall be trials and tribulations, wars, pestilences, signs and wonders, mighty signs! and great wonders, and they shall marvel at these-- yet they have seen nought** unto the glory of the Lord! Behold ye the glory of the Lord!

For I am the Lord thy God

Sananda Son of God the Father

* After this present mission is finished

** Which can compare with....-.

Truth

Mine beloved ones- the hand of God writes within the eth and thou art privileged to be the readers thereof- for I say unto thee look! See! Behold! that which is written therein- not one word is out of place, or time- the "WORD" which is written therein shall be translated into thine own language and written upon thine heart that no man taketh it from thee- I say let no Man despoil it for thee- for it is given unto many to add too and take away -

I say: unto them which hath- shall be added unto--

So let it be the real- that which is true as it is given forth from the mouth of God- pure in thought and manifestation for this hast it been sent forth-

I am the Lord thy God- sent that ye might have the word- and be ye as ones which have it in its pristine purity- let not one letter be added to or taken away- for there are none so sad as the one which betrays himself- Be ye as ones true unto thine calling--

I Am Sananda

Recorded by Thedra

The Goddess of Love

Borea: Mine blessings I would bestow upon thee this day- I would speak unto thee of love, for am I not referred to as the Goddess of love? I say this is an honor bestowed upon Me by Mine own which have worked unceasingly lo the eons of time- this office which I now hold is one of the most important- for it is said, "love cureth all ills, all that which besets mankind" and yet they know not that they do <u>not</u> love! They <u>think</u> themself good! and it is fortuned unto Me to see them reviling against one another and clamoring for peace! poor disillusioned mortals!

I say unto thee they have little knowledge of peace- they long for security and self-satisfaction knowing not from whence cometh their security- I say they cry out in vain for peace- without it is first established within them- for peace is that which has no hatred, no animosity- peace is PEACE! And anything unlike it is the opposite-

It is not given unto Me to go into the places wherein they revile against one another and close out the light-

I say wherein there is one small child which knoweth love- there I am to assist- for I say love is love and brings back its own likeness, for this do I say unto thee- Love them which revile against thee, for thine own sake shall ye love them, it is the law, it returns unto thee bearing its likeness- let it multiply until thine measure swells and runs over that all might partake thereof- let it swell to the brim and spill over- I say they shall come to bathe in the overflow-

So be it I shall speak again and again- I am with thee unto the end- I bless thee with Mine own being- Mine presence-

I Am Borea

Recorded by Thedra

Remembrance: The Benefactors - Sick...

Beloved ones, mighty is the hand of God the Father- and perfect is His work and the manifestation thereof - I say unto thee- be ye as the hand and the foot of Him made manifest upon the Earth- for hast thou not gone forth as His manifestation? I say, thou hast gone forth as ones pure in thine origin - and pure shall ye return unto Him- for I say thine world is as the purifying crucible and purified shall they be which pass through the crucible- for the flame therein shall be as the purifying agent- the flame shall burn away all the dross and the pure shall remain- I say unto thee, the <u>pure</u> only shall remain--

Now let it be said, that the first order of the day is devotion unto the Lord God- Unto the Father Solen Aum Solen first and last- yet unto Him all the praise and the Glory- and forget not thine benefactors, for them* art thou sustained-

I say unto thee remember the sick and the tormented and bless them as ye would be blest- I speak this day of remembrance- and let it be for this that I speak that ye forget not that I am with thee- I am

Sananda

* Because of them- thru them.

Recorded by Thedra

The Compound & Traitors

Beloved of Mine being- be ye blest this day- and say unto them as I would say: that when it is come that they go so far as to jeopardize the safety of the planet Earth, they shall be as ones bound and put into a compound- and they shall remain for a time wherein they shall learn well the lesson which they have spurned so long- I say: they shall be bound and put into a compound wherein they shall learn well the lesson so long spurned- while it is given unto Me to work for many a millennium for the planet Earth - I say that We, the hierarchy shall <u>not</u> allow her to be sacrificed!! I say this with no scorn for them which betray themself of their trust- yet I say it with great compassion for them for I know that condition called the "compound" wherein they do <u>perish</u> a <u>thousand times</u> over- and no relief cometh when they call.

For in no way have they fortuned unto themself relief- they have fortuned such unto themself; and the pity of it. They know not the suffering they bring upon themself- they plunge headlong into their experiments and their own willful actions shall bring about their own destruction- the destruction of their hand work- all their plans, and their physical bodies-.

Once they have destroyed their bodies they go into greatest bondage- wherein they shall groan in agony for a great period of time and therein they shall die a thousand times over- Great suffering- and remorse shall they endure and great shall be their cries for mercy- while the gates shall be closed against them- for a period of time they shall wail- and call- and be as ones cut off - this is not a joyful aspect of Mine instructions unto them- yet the times are precarious and thou art one of Mine servants- I ask of thee be ye as Mine handmade manifest unto them and give unto them this word- and appraise them of their part - their obligation and their duty-.

For it is the obligation of each and every man given breath of life to uphold the dignity of man and walk upright in the way set before him- for he hast had the law clearly given unto him- he no longer can plead ignorance of the law- for it is given unto us to see that they have the law given unto them! They know that which they do to be evil! I say we shall not stand by and suffer our hand work to go for nought!

Now that I have spoken out frankly and fearlessly- ye shall give it unto them in like manner and I shall be unto thee thine shield and thine buckler- wait not for any man's sanction or approval- keep thine own counsel and I shall be with thee- I Am

Sanat Kumara

Recorded by Thedra

The Aggressor (War Mongers)

This day I would say unto thee hold high Mine lamp; and give unto them this word, as it is given unto thee- it is now time for a great revelation of the reality which shall bring unto them great light-- for it is time that they know wherein they are staid. I say they shall come to know that which is hidden from them- for this do I speak out this day. Now it is given unto them to deny Me--

Mine existence-- Mine teaching-- and they dare defy the law- the law which has been given unto them from the beginning - the law which says- "love ye one another-- thou shall not kill- love thine neighbor as thine self"- these things have they ignored! these things they do not! and I say unto them be ye as ones which fan the coals for thine own feet for ye shall walk upon them- ye shall drink of the poison cup which thou hast prepared for thine brother- enemy! sayest thou-- I ask of thee art thou friend when thou prepare a lair for thine brothers- what is this friend or foe? wherein is there justice and mercy amongst them? I say they are traitors and they shall be dealt with justly- so be it I am not the judge- yet I know the law--.

Now I say unto thee, ye which have a mind to follow where I lead thee-- pray for them-- love them- yet ye shall be no part of their foolishness- their hypocrisy, for they make a mockery of that which they call righteousness-- they are not righteous! they are as the traitors and worse than infidels- they are hypocrites- they are as a stench unto Me-- for I know them for that which they are.

They are not the CHRISTians -- the loyalists-- the Godly Saints they professed to be-- I say they stand with bloodstained hands, and they shall be held accountable unto the law-- so be it I have spoken out against them- so be it I shall set Mine hand against them and they shall be put to the end- there shall be an end to the aggressor- the aggression- be it where it may - it shall end - so let it be according unto the will of the Father which hast sent Me--.

For I am come that there be light- So let it be--.

I AM Sananda -

Recorded by Thedra

Changes

Beloved ones: The day comes when there shall be great joy and peace amongst Mine children- for I shall bring them out of the chaotic world wherein they have had no rest-

I say they shall find peace- for this do I say "follow ye Me that where I go ye might go also".

Now it is come when there shall be great winds and the fires shall take their toll and the planes of the air shall fall- and no place can they find security- yet I say unto them behold the hand of God moveth for it shall bring to pass that which is written- it shall sweep clean the debris which is carried over from ages past- it shall remove the <u>OLD</u> and make way for the new-

I say the old shall pass and all shall be made new- the old shall give way to the new- for therein is wisdom- I say the Father's plan is perfect- and all which doth oppose it shall be removed as by natural law-

Now let it be established this day that all which pass from the vehicle of flesh are not condemned- neither are they of darkness- for I have said, they shall step from their dense body into their body of light substance as ones glorified, purified and justified- so be it that ye shall remember that there is no death- there is change and change is good- so be it there shall be great changes- lament them not! for all things shall change with the exception of the law which provides the change-

So be ye as ones prepared- and be at peace and poise- and I shall attend thee-

For I am the Lord thy God

Sananda

Recorded by Thedra

Solen Aum Solen

Mine beloved children: while it is given unto thee to be as ones bound in flesh- I say unto thee thou art not flesh- thou art spirit- flesh is that which is animated by spirit- flesh passeth away - spirit is eternal- life eternal- without end for thou art of Me- sent forth as Mine own self made flesh- I say I have taken form in flesh- and I have given of Mine self that I might have form, form of flesh- any form which I shall take upon Mineself I call perfect-

Yet I say that form which thou seest is not that which I gave unto thee in the beginning- for that form is a perfect one and again ye shall claim it and use it, for it is intact- yet the one which thou seest is not a resemblance of the perfection which thou didst go out with in the beginning- I say the first form which thou didst have was perfect in its manifestation, thou hast wandered long in bondage- making for thine self poor images of the thine self- thine real self- which is perfect--

I say thou art perfect in thine origin- yet thou hast gathered unto thineself a poor likeness of thine real self, thine true self- I say unto thee thou art children of light substance and of the light art thou created for I am the light- I AM that I AM and I diminish not by or because of Mine creation- I say I create perfectly and for this I say ye shall return unto Me perfect even as ye went out- so be it I have given unto thee one fiat "return unto Me this day and be ye made whole"

I Am thine Father

Solen Aum Solen

Recorded by Thedra

First Born / Spores / Whores

Beloved children while it is yet time I say unto thee give unto Me credit for knowing thine every need- thine every want- and give unto Me credit for being that which I am- for I say unto thee thine needs shall be supplied and thine hands shall be Mine hands and thine feet Mine feet- for I say unto thee thou art Mine: for have I not sent thee forth as Mine own self, made flesh? I say as Mine own self have I made thee manifest- for thou art Me- born of Me- because of Me thou art and I say unto thee thou art of the first born- the <u>first</u> <u>born</u>- born of spirit and not any place wherein I am do I find a spore. Spores they create- whores the spores create, and I say unto thee thou art of the first born- wherein is there a spore or a whore amongst the first born?

I speak unto thee of things which they know not- yet they shall come to know- for it is said that which is hidden shall be revealed- so it shall be-

I Am thine Father

Solen Aum Solen

The Use of the Words Solen Aum Solen

Holy Holy is the name of Solen Aum Solen- remember it and speak it with reverence- keep it before thee, and know that there is power in the word- keep it within thine heart and adore the name, for it is given unto thee that ye be lifted up- use it not blasphemously- use it not without thought for I say unto thee there is power in the word and it shall bless thee- for this hast it been revealed unto thee- Keep it sacred--

I say unto thee the time is come when ye shall behold the power of the word- ye shall see it manifest before thee, for the time is now come when the spoken word shall bring forth fruit now- it shall be as the twinkling of an eye- when the word shall bring forth instant fruit- no longer shall ye wait for the word to go out and return - it shall bring back the fruits thereof instantaneously - for it shall be done, that which goes out from thy mouth shall bring results instantly and ye shall see the fruits thereof-

I say unto thee be ye as ones prepared for this is Mine word unto thee this day- hold thine peace and give unto thine self no bitter cup- for I say ye shall drink of the cup which ye prepare for thine brother--

So let it be sweet-

I Am thine older brother

Sananda

Recorded by Thedra

The Day of the Lord is Come

Beloved ones- this day I would give unto thee this word- be ye as the hand and foot of Me- for I say unto thee ye shall do Mine work, ye shall do that which shall be portioned out for thee with joy and thanksgiving- ye shall be unto Me Mine handmaidens for I say without these I am not sufficient - for this have I called thee out from them which have not given unto Me credit for being that which I am- I say I have revealed Mineself unto thee and given unto thee a part separate from theirs- yet it is for the good of all that I reveal Mineself at this time- I say they shall come to know that I Am- and they shall not deny Me, for I am the Lord thy God, sent of Mine Father that this day might bring forth <u>NEW FRUIT</u>- and it is said it shall be of a different variety- for I say it shall be different from anything which they have known-

Now I say unto them - all which have held steadfast shall be glad this day is come- they shall be as ones rewarded; for all their waiting shall end- it is come when they which have served Me diligently shall be caught up with Me and they shall rejoice and be glad- while the traitors shall run hither and yon lamenting their unknowing- and they shall fall down and cry Lord, Lord hast thou forsaken us? They shall declare their love and loyalty after they have seen the folly of their ways- they shall see the doors close upon them- and there shall be great sorrow and confusion. These shall be the ones which have <u>betrayed themself</u>-

And now I say unto thee- be ye not so foolish as to deny Me- and that which I do- for I am sent that Mine Father be glorified in the Earth as He is in the heavens- be ye as ones alert and hasten thee to set thine house in order and be ye prepared for the day of the Lord is at hand- I say the day of the Lord is come when I shall gather Mine own unto

Mineself, and I shall show Mine hand- make ye haste and prepare thineself- for I am come that ye might have light- that where I go ye might go also- so let it be as the Father hast willed it- I say unto thee Mine beloved ye shall give this unto them which are yet bound in bondage; darkness and they shall receive it in Mine name. So be it-

I am Sananda Son of God-

Recorded by Sister Thedra

Preparation Is Becoming

Blest are they which ask of Me that they might have light, so let it be- for this have I revealed Mineself-

Now I say unto thee there is no other way unto, or into the Father's kingdom save by Me- I am the door, I am the way- and I am not unmindful of the cry of the soul- I am aware of all thine anguish, thine cries, thine every need- yet I say unto thee the preparation hast many sides, many facets- for the first is obedience unto the law- the law hast been given and it is exacting- the mind to learn is one- the love one for the other is <u>not</u> least- the <u>greatest</u> is <u>love</u>- and there are all the virtues which shall be part of thee- these shall make up the character of the initiate, these shall be his very being- and not one of the virtues shall be omitted for he shall not deceive himself-

I say preparation is becoming that which thou hast "willed". Thou art this day that which ye have "willed" thineself to be.

Thine waiting hast been long and hard- yet for thine own sake hast it been- there is the preparation which the initiate goes through to prepare him for the next place wherein he shall go- and that which shall be given unto him to do- which pertains to the greater part- the place wherein he shall go after he steps from his dense body of earthly substance- he shall be aware of his place, and he shall be prepared for it and he shall know and know that he knows- he shall be as one come alive- he shall not see death, for it shall be no part of him.

He shall be prepared for his light body and he shall have no fear - for he shall be prepared-

While I say unto thee there are many ways in which thou art prepared for the greater part, I say first ye shall will to be prepared- with the will to follow where I lead thee- that where I go ye shall go also- there is the action to be taken- the will to do- to become, to be. The becoming is the change of the old nature, the human nature into that of the divine- this is the long sought path wherein thou dost become the illumined being known as "Son of God" this is the way- the life- this is the path of the initiate where one becomes- that which is the overcoming is thine preparation-

I say unto thee "come ye out from among them". Be ye no part of the hypocrites and infidels- for I say unto thee deceive **NOT** thineself- search within thine closet for that which thou hast hidden therein through the ages past- forgive thineself- and cast it from thee- and remember it no more- for therein is freedom- freedom which ye know not of- hear that which I say unto thee and be ye as one glad- for I have spoken that it be so- be ye blest of Me and by Me for I am come that ye be blest-

I Am the Lord thy God

Sananda

Recorded by Sister Thedra

In That Day...

Mine beloved ones- The day shall bring forth great light- for it is now come when great revelation shall be given unto them which are prepared to receive, I say that this is the day of revelation, and great light shall be shed upon them which are prepared to receive of it- too I say that they which doth receive of it shall be truly blest--

Mine time is come when I shall gather Mine sheep and I shall give unto them that which I have kept for them- this is their inheritance- this is that which the Father hast willed unto them-

Now I say unto thee the time is come when ye shall be as ones prepared for the greater part- "the part which is kept for thee".

So be it there shall be the ones which have not been true unto themself and these shall cry out for mercy and deliverance- they shall wander to and fro lamenting their unknowing- yet I have given unto them the law- the word, which they have rejected- so be it they shall cry out Lord, Lord here I am bring, me out- yet it is said there is a time unto all things- and I say unto them make ye haste this day that ye might be prepared to go where I go- yet they believe Me not- and it shall be their own sorrow- and undoing- for the gate shall close upon them and they shall wait- they shall wait for another day- and their waiting shall be long and hard-

Yet, I say unto them which believeth upon Me- these shall I bring out in that day of great sorrow and wailing- and these shall rejoice for their preparation, so be it a glad day for them which follow Me for they shall find peace--.

So be it I Am Sananda

Recorded by Sister Thedra

The Word of the Lord

This day I would say unto thee be ye as Mine hand and Mine feet made manifest upon the Earth- and go ye forth as sons of God, which thou art, and give unto them this word, and declare unto them that I am come, the Lord thy God- and give unto them that which I give unto thee for them- and bless them as ye would be blest- and forget not the sick and the dying- so shall ye remember them which art amongst the dead- I say, ye shall remember them which are <u>bound</u> in darkness, pray for them that thine light go out that it might be seen by them that thy light might be a beacon unto their feet-

So be it that many sleepeth this day which shall awaken this day; they shall hear the voice of the Lord thy God- for I shall raise Mine voice that they might hear- I say unto them; "come ye forth, come ye alive, awaken and come forth from amongst the dead!" hear ye that which I say unto them which sleepeth- and be ye as Mine hand and

Mine foot made manifest unto the living dead which walketh amongst thee.

I say unto "them" awaken from thine sleep- thine lethargy, and come alive, follow ye Me, that where I go ye might go also- and be ye as ones blest forevermore- let this be unto thee the word of the Lord- and hear ye Me, for I have spoken this day that ye might have light- that ye might come alive, and be brought out of bondage, so be it for thine own sake that I have come into the Earth; that there be light.

It is now time that there be light- for darkness hast descended upon Mine people, and they have forgotten their origin and they know not whither they goest- I say, it is now time they awaken- for the day swiftly cometh when I shall call their name, and they shall be as the ones prepared, or they shall be as ones yet asleep, and the ones asleep shall be confused, they shall run within the streets as wild beasts crying- WHITHER! WHITHER! as they shall be as ones lost- for the ones which are awakened and have kept their covenant with Me shall be taken and they shall be left to their sorrowful plight- I call unto them yet they deny Me, they heed not Mine voice, these are the laggards, and the traitors- I say there are none so sad as them which betray themself; these are the pitiful ones.

Now I say unto thee: go ye forth and declare unto them I am come that they be brought out before the day of sorrow- so let it be that I am with thee that ye might <u>know</u> that I am-

I Am that I Am, The Lord thy God

Sananda

Recorded by Sister Thedra

Father

O, Mighty, Allwise Father Solen Aum Solen, know ye all that we are, all that we shall become, know ye our beginning our end - from thee cometh all our blessings- all that we have or shall ever have is because of thee- unto thee all praise all glory- for Father thou art all that we thine sons desire- let thine being be unto us our refuge, our strength, our all--

For thou hast sent us forth as thyself made manifest in flesh. I say, O Father I am come into the Earth made manifest as flesh- animated by the end. Thee, O, Father give unto them strength and peace and the knowing which is Mine- be they blest as I am blest- let them drink from the fount of thine eternal love- the fount which springs eternal- and let them be filled and satisfied- for this do I pray thee Father- let this thine Son be unto thee thine hand and thine foot- for their sake do I speak unto thee this day in words of theirs that they might come to know the oneness which we share-

O Father, let their hearts swell with love one for the other and bring themself unto thine dwelling place in the end-

So let it be as thou hast willed it-

I Am thine Son

Sananda

Recorded by Sister Thedra

See God's Hand Move

This day I would say unto thee "Look, See", see the mighty work which I shall do-

For I say unto thee the hand of God shall sweep clean all that which doth oppose the light; for it is power, it is truth and justice- I say <u>nothing</u> which doth oppose it shall stand. For it is now come when the Earth shall be prepared for her new place within the firmaments- and she shall find her place and she shall fill it as planned in the beginning- she shall be as the shining orb she was created-

Now I say unto thee: the Sons of God shall stand arrayed in their seamless garments and they shall be as the "Sons of God" sent forth that this time, this age bring forth the harvest- for it is the time long prophesied- it was told of old that this would come-

Yet, there are ones which know it not: for they are of the old order- they have not the mind to learn- neither the mind to comprehend- I say unto thee these shall be as the ones opinionated- they shall be as the ones which <u>think</u> themself wise! And they shall be confronted with their foolishness- they shall cry out Lord! Lord! Have mercy on us. hast thou forsaken us?

These shall be as ones left- these shall wait another day- and their waiting shall be long and hard- I have cried unto them: prepare! prepare! prepare thineself for the day cometh when no man shall sleep- for they shall have no place wherein to lay their head- they shall be as the foxes- they shall burrow into the ground and be glad for the shelter- I say they which have betrayed themself shall know great sorrow-

They shall learn! For it is the LAW-

I say unto them: be ye as ones prepared that ye might be lifted up- so be it I am the Lord thy God sent of Mine Father that it be so- so let it be-

I Am Sananda

Recorded by Sister Thedra

Ye Shall Not...

Beloved ones- while thou knowest not the fullness of the 'great plan' I say unto thee thou art part of it- for were it not so I should not reveal unto thee Mine prospectus- Mine word- Mineself- I should not speak at this time. Yet it is appropriate that I do so- NOW!

While it is yet time I say unto thee, give unto them which art yet in darkness that the day draws nigh when the sun shall be blotted out and they shall be without light for a time, and they shall be as ones powerless- they shall be helpless- for they shall be caught unaware- they have been warned- yet they heed not- they go headlong into battle, they give unto their fellow man the bitter cup- they give of themself unto the dragon that his nefarious schemes be accomplished- they know Me not! they ask not of the Father which hast given unto them being! they are under the hood- the <u>black</u> hood, they hear not - neither do they see- they ask not for deliverance of the Father- they ask of man which is likewise entrapped, ensnared- I say they are entrapped- and they know not which way to turn. <u>Some</u> say there is no escape- others say it is the Father's will- others say, it is the only way-

I say unto them: be ye not deceived- for the Father hast <u>NOT</u> willed it thus- I say unto thee: "thou shall not kill- neither shall ye take up arms against thine fellow man-" I say, ye shall not plunder- neither exploit him or impoverish him- ye shall be as ones which have upon thine own shoulders the responsibility of thine own salvation and <u>each</u> shall be <u>accountable</u> for his own salvation of himself, his family, and <u>his country</u>- I say thou shall not trespass upon each other- ye shall not transgress the law- unseen- unknown- uncensored, for the law is just and exacting- it plays no favorites- ye shall not be as ones blinded by thine own will, by thine own opinions, and conceit.

I say unto thee bind up the wounds which thou hast inflicted and make ye haste to set thine house in order: for the day draws nigh when ye shall cry out for mercy, strength and light, and I shall say unto thee- it is late and thou hast wasted thine inheritance- be ye gone- thou hast not known Me- for I have been unto thee a just and faithful servant- I have stood by in peace, and I have offered thee a hand and thou wastral thou hast spit upon it and rejected it, thou hast denied Me and that which I have proffered unto thee, now ye shall prepare thineself for a new part and a new place wherein ye shall learn the hard way- so be it I know the law- for this do I speak out this day that ye might be prepared- so be it.

I am the Lord thy God

Sananda

Recorded by Sister Thedra

Sananda's Prayer to The Father

Mighty Father, most blessed, we ask for these thine children that they might know the cause of their being- the source of their being- as we the illumined of thee, for this do I give unto them as they are able to comprehend- now I say unto them: "be ye at peace and poise, let nothing be unto thee a tack in thine shoe" yet they are as the little ones, they have not as yet comprehended the fullness of Mine words- for they trouble themself of small matters-

I say they weary of small things and they are weary of body and they have the heaviness of flesh upon them- yet I give of Mineself that the spirt be refreshed, and vitalized- I give of Mine love and wisdom that they might be led aright-- Now I ask of thee that they be quickened of spirit, strengthened and revitalized of body and be brought to the fulfillment of their mission upon the Earth, and received at last into the holy of holies- so let it be as thou hast willed it--

Thank thee adorable Father, I adore thee

Sananda

Beloved, it is Mine time- and I say unto thee ye shall be as one which has the place and the will to do Mine work-ye shall place before them this word and it shall serve them well- for it is now come when ye shall be given a greater part- ye shall be prepared in the place wherein ye are and ye shall be as one blest, for it is given unto Me to know that which thou hast done- and shall do- yet it is not finished-

I say that there shall be ones which have the will to assist thee and they shall be blest in the doing- while it is yet time, I say unto thee ye shall finish the place wherein ye shall rest and be at peace, separate from the brothers and the others for that which shall be given unto thee to do- the time shall be allotted for this and it shall be for the good of all- the ones which stand ready to assist shall be the ones prepared for a part and they shall give of their substance in return for thine faithful service-

Now let it be said that not one goes unrewarded- unseen- unnoticed, for I am not asleep- neither do I fail Mine part for I am not a traitor- I am not finished, I am alert and ready to finish that which I have begun-

So be it I am the Lord thy God

Recorded by Sister Thedra

Gather Together Thine Self....

Mine children- when thou went out from Me thou wast perfect of form and thou didst know from whence thou came- thou didst know that when ye went from thine place of abode thou wouldst forfeit thine inheritance for a time-

I say it hast been long that thou hast been away from thine abiding place- yet it is now come when ye shall return unto it as ones prepared- I say as ones prepared ye shall return unto Me- with great joy ye shall be received and there shall be great joy throughout the cosmos that this day is come-

Now I say unto thee thine time is come- thine hour has come when ye shall gather thineself and return unto Me- for this have I sent Mine

Son unto thee that it be so- so let it be- for this have I given unto thee the command; "return unto me and be made whole"- So let it be-

I Am thine Father

Solen Aum Solen

Interpretation...

Mine beloved children, I have given unto thee life- life of Mine life- I have sent thee forth as Mineself- as Mine hand and Mine foot made manifest upon Earth that I Might have the place upon Earth as Mine- Mineself made flesh have I placed upon the Earth- and I have walked in flesh, flesh of Mine flesh, animated by spirit- spirit of Mine spirit.

Now I say unto thee, it is come when ye shall come to know that thou art one with Me, ye shall come to remember thine origin and ye shall return unto it- for have I not provided for it- thine return?-

I say unto thee ye <u>shall</u> return into thine abiding place- and therein ye shall know- ye shall know as I know- for this do I speak unto thee thusly- now ye shall record that which hast been given unto thee in symbolic form and it shall be for the good of all, for I say unto thee it is now come when the records shall be revealed and the secrets shall be revealed unto them- let no man put upon these revelations his own "interpretations", rather, ask of the Father for light and it shall not be denied him-

I am He which giveth and taketh away-

I Am

Solen Aum Solen

Recorded by Sister Thedra

Faithfulness

Beloved ones, this day I would speak unto thee of faithfulness, that which is prompted by love, and loyalty, for it is given unto Me to seek out the faithful ones which would serve Me, and which would be unto Me Mine hands and Mine feet- I say unto these which would be unto Me Mine servants, they shall be tested for their mettle, their strength of character, their loyalty and faithfulness- for is not loyalty and faithfulness one with love? And is this not the character: strength which is necessary for the building material of Mine house- "The Temple of the Lord in which I shall dwell"? I say I am the Lord, and I choose Mine building material carefully- I am not deceived for I am a builder- I build well, and I build not on quicksand- I say I build upon the rock which I AM, and I am not swayed by the foul winds which blow unto the four corners of the Earth, I say I am <u>firm</u> and I know that which I am about, and I go not out- neither do I come for I Am that I Am, I speak the "Word" and it is apparent that which I have spoken- I am not want to deceive Mineself for I am not so foolish-

Now I say unto them which have set their course unto or by the <u>great star</u>, fear not for I am with thee and I shall not forsake thee- for I am the Wayshower, I come that ye might find thine way into the inner temple- so be it ye shall follow where I lead thee and great shall be thine joy, I say, great shall be thine reward for ye knoweth not that which is in store for thee, for it hast not <u>as</u> <u>yet</u> been revealed unto thee, not all thine imaging could be unto thee as great, not all thine opinions shall be unto thee wisdom- I say thine own opinions shall be as nought- for they shall be as legirons which shall be cast off- put aside and be no more- I say therein shall be freedom, drag them not- for therein is bondage- I say free thine self of thine legirons- let them Go! for they shall serve to hold thee captive! I come that ye might have light- So let it be as ye will it- it is now come when ye shall accept it and be free- or ye shall remain the captive in bondage-

I have spoken, yet I am not through-

I AM

Sananda

Recorded by Sister Thedra

The Presence of the King

I was in a small temple, rustic, sort of a country place, very simple- the King had come amongst us to talk to us. I sat on a front bench, with just a few others, I was unaware of any others behind us.

The King held within his hand a huge book from which he was apparently taking his cue.

He wore a small robe- <u>much</u> too small, striking him just below the elbows and hips- it was not what one would expect the king to wear- it was shoddy- yet did not detract from his station or dignity--

One dignitary sat upon my left- when the King appeared in a very happy, jovial mood- he paid me (Thedra) a compliment- feeling very small and childish in his presence, I cringed, shrunk with embarrassment, and whispered to my escort on the left. "I am getting out of here". He set me at ease by smiling and saying, "you will not go- you will remain- all is well"-

As the King moved about in his rhythmic motion his secrets were exposed- nothing hidden-...

Revelation- Symbolic form-

This will from necessity be given in parts, for it seemed to have no beginning- no end-

I, Thedra was in a great- large place where there was service to be given, such as "trade, exchange" waiting on people etc.

My part appeared to be that of an "extra" and my part was finished, I was aware of not having to punch a time clock- I had to report to the one in charge and turn in my <u>knife</u>, <u>fork</u>, and <u>spoon</u> and my uniform, or "garment" that I wore. I lay down on a bed to fold the robe- garment which I had in my hand, I found it to be a pink clean one which had upon it a medicinal spot, weak or faded out, I called my supervisors attention to it, to which she replied, it is alright that is medicine you are not responsible for it. I realized I had never put that robe on--

Sister Thedra.

Where Does the Responsibility Lie?

Mine children; this day I would say unto thee, thine time is Mine time, the time is allotted unto all things- the sowing, the blooming, the reaping, yea, unto the consuming thereof, I say even unto the consuming thereof-

Now while it is but the seeding time, I say, they shall reap that which they have sown and even now are sowing; the thistles shall spring up as never before in their midst and the thorns shall be mighty spears which shall rend their flesh, and they shall cry out for mercy- I say they shall cry out for mercy, and they shall find none- until they have consumed all their own misused energy and transmuted it for the good of all-

Now they have tasted of the bitter cup which they have prepared for another- yet I say they shall drink unto the last drop- for it is the law- and it is said, place before them the "word" and they shall be responsible for that which they do with it- so be it the responsibility shall weigh heavy upon them-

I am come that they might have light and I find no light within "them" for they are as the bigots, and the traitors, they betray themself and they know it not! Yet, I say, unto them- be ye aware of thine own shortcomings and hasten to set thine own house in order- give unto thine brothers not the bitter cup-

I am not asleep- I see and know that which goes on behind their locked doors and that which is within their heart- I say- each one is responsible for his part- and each one is responsible for his own salvation; for his own legirons which he now fashions for himself-

I say, cut them away! And begin this day to set thine own house in order- and ye shall profit thereby- so be it I have spoken and I am not finished!

I Am the Lord thy God

Sananda

Recorded by Sister Thedra

Them Which Doth Obey the Law...

Mine hand shall be as a mighty rod, and as a power in the land- and on the sea, and I shall be unto them which doth obey the law a mighty shield and a light- they shall be upheld in their judgment, for they shall judge righteous judgment- they shall be given the power to distinguish the true from the false- they shall know the antichrists and they shall be as ones prepared to deal wisely with them- they shall uphold the law of righteousness and they shall not fail- they shall know the truth and it shall set them free for I say they shall uphold the law and they shall deal justly with their fellow men- they shall be honorable in the place wherein they labor for bread and they shall practice the law of righteousness and no hypocrisy shall be within them- they shall be bold in their righteousness, and no fear shall they know, they shall stand firm as the rock which I am- they shall not weary of well doing- and they shall be humble in their labors and gentle of speech, they shall not boast of their powers and good deeds, for they shall know wherein they are staid- they shall give credit where credit is due and they shall be found worthy of their calling--

I say unto them: weary not, for I am with thee that it be finished- I am come that it be finished and the house of the Lord shall be filled with rejoicing when it is done- I say unto them which labor without ceasing be ye as ones blest, for thine labor shall bring forth great reward- and ye shall be as ones blest-

Be it so- that ye which labor for bread shall eat thereof- yet these which labor for peace and justice shall eat thereof and greater shall be his reward- for he shall hunger no more--

I Am the Lord thy God

Sananda

Recorded By Sister Thedra

THIS RESURRECTION

The Awakening

Mine children, this is the time of awakening, the time of "<u>awakening</u>" when all things shall throw off the old and take on the new -- the resurrection is now this day, and shall be the next and the next, for there shall be yet other days of resurrection, when yet greater awakening shall be given and the time for <u>this</u> resurrection is now this day- and it is now come that there shall be a great awakening and many shall be as ones resurrected from the dead- "the <u>living</u> dead", they shall be lifted up, and they shall come alive, and they shall walk upright- knowing whither they goest and from whence they came-

Now I say unto them: "it is the way of the dragon to try to rob thee of thine inheritance", yet I come that ye be prepared to receive it, and I tell thee of a surety that there is a place prepared for thee and it is my part to show the way, <u>yet</u>, it is thine part to follow after Me that where I go ye might go also-

Ye shall be as ones prepared for I say, each shall be put into his own environment and it behooves thee to be prepared that ye be put in a place of light, and peace, wherein there is no darkness-- too, I say, ye shall put aside all thine preconceived ideas of Me and about Me- and ask of the Father light, and it shall be given unto thee-- yet ye shall not make for thineself any "images". Ye shall clean away all thine false images and replace them not! for I say unto thee, <u>mortal</u> <u>man</u> hast not the mind to comprehend the fullness of the plan- the great and divine plan which is NOW in operation- I say, "it is <u>NOW</u> in operation" and ye sleepeth still, knowing not-- thou seeest as through a mist, the veil of Maya. Yet I say it shall be rent asunder- and ye shall see as with eyes of spirit, and then ye shall know for a surety- and ye shall not be deceived- so be it I am come that ye might know- hope is born of faith, faith is born of a secret knowing- yet I say all these things shall be revealed unto them which follow Me-.

I bid thee come - I say unto thee awaken, be ye as ones come alive, arise with Me, that where I go ye might go also, such is Mine word unto thee at this season- peace, peace, peace-.

Sananda

Recorded by Sister Thedra

Preparation and Environment

Say unto them in Mine name that there is a mighty and powerful host which awaits to deliver them up- and they shall be as the ones prepared for the places where in they shall be put- I say they shall each be put into the place where they are in their own environment, they shall be in the place they have prepared for themself - I say they shall be in their own environment-

Now I say to the warrior he shall find himself a warrior still, for he shall be in his own environment- the peacemaker shall find himself in a place wherein he shall be at peace- I say each in his own environment- that which he has created for himself- this is the word which I would give unto them this day- prepare thineself for the greater part- for I say the day cometh when no man shall sleep- for this is the time of awakening- for this Am I come- I come that they be awakened-

Now they shall run hither and yon asking of men, yet I say the responsibility rests upon their own shoulders- and they shall make their own decisions which they choose- I say; "choose ye this day which way ye go"- Too I say, blessed is the peacemaker- I say let peace first be established within thine own heart- love ye one another- bless thine ownself in the doing- be ye alert and give no man the bitter cup- rest in the case knowing that the law is just- and merciful- and betray not thine ownself- for this have I given unto thee the law- the key- I say ye have but to apply the law unto thine ownself- which turns the key into the inner temple- wherein these things shall be revealed unto thee which have mystified thee- be ye prepared for the great learning which is not of men and their opinions- seek not of men and their opinions for therein is an error- I am come that there be light- so let it be- for I say unto thee all which doth oppose it shall be removed by natural law- such is Mine word unto thee this day-

I am Sananda the Lord God

Recorded by Sister Thedra

The Fullness of Thine Inheritance

While it is given unto Me to be the Lord thy God, I say unto thee thou art sons of God the Father, born of Him, born of the spoken word and He, the Father, hast given unto thee life, life of His life and He hast given unto thee the mind and the power that ye might comprehend the greater things and it is for this that I have revealed Mineself unto thee- I say it is because of this that I have given of Mineself that ye might be as ones for the greater part which is the fullness of thine inheritance-

Now ye have drunken of the dregs of thine cup- thou hast eaten of the tree of knowledge and thou hast not remembered that which thou hast known- I say thou hast not remembered that which thou hast done: yet I say thou hast been of many minds- many bodies hast thou taken unto thineself- yet ye know not the fullness of thine existence-

I say unto thee thou art eternal beings; thou art as ones born out of the Eternal parent; of Him born: of Him created - yet that which is eternal hast no beginning, no end- yet thine forms hast been many and varied in shape and likeness- yet the eternal part of thee changeth not- for it is divine in its origin- and it has not lost its divinity, neither its splendor, for*the going into bondage- I say unto thee ye shall return unto thine abiding place as ones prepared as ones cleansed- purified and the justified- unscathed- unharmed- and ye shall remember that which thou hast done- wherein thou hast been- and that which hast been accomplished- so be it that I am the Lord thy God.

Sananda

* Because of going into bondage.

Recorded by Sister Thedra

The Day of Gathering

Beloved: It is now time to speak of the great day when there shall be the gathering in. It is not a day of succor, it is not a time of comfort, it is the time of sifting and sorting, the bringing out the ones of divine origin, the ones which have taken unto themself bodies of flesh for the purpose of finding the others which have come so long ago, which have forgotten their way, forgotten their identity- the ones which have searched for the lost ones.

I say unto thee none are lost from Mine sight- they are lost from themself simply because they have forgotten their source- I say their memory hast been blanked from them, they are as ones with amnesia, yet they shall be caused to remember their identity- for they shall be touched and they shall have their memory restored unto them- I say they shall be <u>made</u> to remember- for this have I said "they shall know as I know"- so be it a glad day when the veil is torn asunder and they shall rejoice that it is finished, their wanderings- I say it shall end and they shall rejoice, so be it and Selah--.

Now I speak unto thee of the day when they shall be gathered from the four corners of the Earth- there are many which have come as emissaries which have fallen asleep, and they shall be awakened, for these shall be the first to awaken, and then the second shall be the ones of the first born- and they shall in turn serve to awaken the ones which have come from other realms, which are of another order- these which are of the first born shall serve to lift <u>them</u> up and bring <u>them</u> out, and so shall they too become sons of God in their time which is allotted unto them- I say these shall too become of the highest order- and they shall come into the place provided for them: and it is said each unto his season, each unto his own time.

So be it truth for none shall be brought out prematurely- I say, <u>NONE</u> shall be brought out prematurely- yet there shall be a place for each, provided for him as he is prepared- there shall be no 'misfits' for each unto his own and according unto his preparation and in his own order- I say each in his place, and in his own order- none shall be out of place, for all is according to order and within the law- for none is overlooked- none <u>missed</u>!

I am within the place wherein there is light- for I am light and within the place wherein I am is but love and light- yet the children of Earth know but little of either love or light- which is one- the same- yet unknown in its entirety or perfection- the love which they know is a poor counterfeit for the perfect love which is ours- I say for our love we have watched- guarded, counseled, and Sibored them lo, the eons of time that they have wandered in bondage, for we forget not our own*- for this have we worked without ceasing that they might return unto their abiding place-

Now I say unto them arise! Come home, come home, let thine wanderings end- and receive thine inheritance in full- and give unto the Father all the credit and the glory, praise ye His holy name- and receive of Him thine gift of eternal life-

So be it I have spoken that they might know that which enables them to awaken- for this have I spoken simply and in parables**- yet truly so. So be it as the Father hast willed it-

I Am that I Am

* Because they are of one order.

** So much here revealed in spirit- which cannot be put into any language- even the parables are insufficient. (Thedra)

The Law of Cause and Effect

Mighty is the hand of God, and great power is within it- I say, there is great power within the hand of God- see it move, see the word made manifest- for I say unto thee "the word shall be made manifest before thee" and ye shall know that there is peace and justice, and there is a law governing all things- all manifestation- and not one shall escape the law of cause and effect. I say they which have sown unto the winds shall reap the wind, those which have sown unto peace shall reap peace, and these shall each be prepared for the reaping- I say each unto his own--.

Now ye shall place within their hand these Mine words, and I say unto them which are fortuned to read them: Be ye responsible for that which ye sow- and <u>hast</u> <u>sown</u>- for ye shall eat thereof- and it is given unto Me to know each by his own light- I say I shall gather them out from the multitude which serve Me, the light, which I Am- and I shall bring them into the place which is prepared for them and these shall I give unto as they are prepared to receive- I say each shall receive according unto his works- for he which hast sown hatred shall be confronted with his own hatred- he which hast sown love shall find love abounding about him, and he which goes into battle to slay his brother shall be as one in battle- for I have said each in his own environment. Too, I have said the one which loves his fellow man as himself shall be as the one loved- for he has so loved-

Now I say unto them which sit in high places, be ye as ones responsible for thine own part and hold steadfast to truth and justice- betray not thineself nor thine trust- ask of no man aught- keep thine own counsel and be ye as one responsible for such as ye shall be given to do- let no man be unto thee power to shake thine knowing- for I say unto thee, the law hast been given unto thee, ye shall abide thereby and no condemnation shall touch thee, nor tarnish thine armor- for I have said ye shall put on the whole armor of God and nothing shall harm thee-. Be ye mindful of Mine words and be ye as one prepared for great shall be thine responsibility- I have spoken that ye might have knowledge of Mine words, for this have I spoken unto one which hast ears to hear-

I am Sananda the Lord God

Recorded by Sister Thedra

To Them Which Seek High Places of Honor -The Law Is Just

Mine Sibors have I sent unto thee, that ye might have the laws and the light which hast been shed on thee hast been that which thou could take- yet ye have been as children at child's play and it hast not been fully known unto thee the power which is thine; and the power of The W<u>ord</u> which is <u>sufficient to move mountains</u>. I say it is thine greatest asset given to unto thee, the <u>power</u> of The Word, and it is misused; it is given that it which is not prompted by love, neither ethics nor sincerity of purpose is prompted by hypocrisy and worthless in its application- yet it rebounds upon thee causing great confusion and great unrest-

Now ye shall come to know that the <u>law is just</u>, and none escapes it for it is no respecter of persons. I say when ye are given a place wherein ye are to serve, ye shall devote thine whole heart to the work which ye have been given, and for the good of all- and no time shall ye betray thineself- neither thine trust nor perjure thine word - I say the word of thine mouth shall be unto thee sacred, ye shall not be as a liar, ye shall be as one trustworthy in all thine dealings- ye shall be as one responsible for to thine words, thine actions- and ye shall be blest in like measure unto thine works- for I say each shall bear his own responsibility of his work- his own salvation, his family, his country, his people- I say he shall not give unto his fellow men the bitter cup- he shall judge righteous judgment in his dealings- he shall be as the hands and the feet of Me- he shall serve to the greatest light within him- with his whole mind, and heart, he shall make no compromises with the forces of darkness- he shall be as the <u>rock</u>, he shall be unmoved by their ravings and rantings- their <u>hatred</u> shall not touch him- for I say, he shall be as one given the strength and the power to hold his place within his office untouched, unharmed- for I say I shall be unto him his shield and his buckler- I am come that this be brought about- and I say that there shall be great changes made and great shall be the light shed upon the Earth, and Mine servants shall be fortified with the weapons of truth, justice and wisdom- so let it be as the Father hast willed it-

I say all the places wherein they set and plan their nefarious schemes shall be cleaned out; and justice shall prevail- so be it a glad day- I say that oppression shall be no more- and for this do I speak out against them which doth betray themself- and I speak fearlessly and with wisdom-

I say, <u>Unto them which seek high places of honor</u>- be ye not so foolish as to fool thineself, or betray thineself, or thine trust- for thine words shall be unto thee thine own weal or woe- have I not spoken unto thee of the law? hast thou been aware of it in all thine dealings with thine fellow men?

I say unto thee consider well thine intent!

I am now prepared to give unto thee as ye are prepared to receive-

I am the Lord thy God

Sananda

Recorded by Sister Thedra

To Them Which Seek Places of Honor

Behold the works which I shall do, for I say unto thee I shall do a mighty work! I shall put out the ones which have not given of themself unto the light, and I shall place within the places of government them which are one with the light. I shall put them upon the seat of judgment and they shall judge righteous judgment-

I shall give unto them the power and the authority to administer judgment of righteousness. I shall give unto them discernment and I shall favor them- for I say the ones which have tormented Mine people and have harassed them unjustly shall be removed!

I am come that there be light; and justice and mercy is no small part of it- I am now prepared to give unto them according unto their works- I am not deceived by their words- for I am the Lord their God- I say I am not the judge- I know the law- and I say unto them: "I come that it be fulfilled" so shall it be-.

Now ye shall be as ones prepared to stand in the light or ye shall <u>be as ones</u> which has betrayed thineself: for I say great light shall go forth- and it shall remove the darkness- and it shall be for the good of all- I say: "It shall be for the good of all" for I am not of a mind to sacrifice Mine people unto the dragon- I am come that they be unbound, so let it be!

Now while I speak unto them which seek high places of honor, I say they shall be trustworthy in all things, and they shall be prepared, for their responsibility shall weigh heavy upon their shoulders-

Now I say unto them, Mine children hast been burdened by the wayward ones which hast betrayed their trust- they have been persecuted- and crucified! Now ye shall be unto them <u>older brothers</u>, ye shall be as one responsible for thine own self- and for their safety and welfare-

<u>Yet</u>, they shall ask no favors of their government or of the agents thereof- they shall assume the responsibility for themself, and their families- and therein is wisdom- they shall not shift the blame for <u>their short</u>comings <u>onto</u> the shoulders of another-

I say unto the people of the country ye are self-responsible for thine own self and that of thine offspring- ye shall ask of no man to take thine responsibility whether he be of the church or the state- He shall be as the one prepared to take upon himself such responsibility- and he shall not betray himself- for he shall be held responsible-

I speak now of the ones which sit in high places- and mete out the <u>so called</u> "<u>justice</u>" Be ye as ones prepared! For the time cometh when ye shall be judged by the law- I AM THE LAW! And it faileth not!

I speak out that ye might know thine responsibility to be great: I say be ye as ones responsible for all thine actions- let them be according unto the law of justice and be ye prepared for the greater part- And as ye sow so shall ye reap- it is the law- I Am The Wayshower-

The Lord thy God-

Recorded by Sister Thedra

The Law

While it is later than they know- I say it is yet time to turn from their own willfulness and begin their preparation- for the time <u>is</u> <u>come</u> when each shall stand forth and be counted- each shall answer for himself and be accountable for himself, his deeds- his <u>every</u> <u>act</u>- and he shall receive as he hast prepared himself for to receive- I say unto every man, he shall be responsible for his own salvation, for his own redemption- for his misused energy- and he shall atone for all his misdeeds- he shall qualify himself to enter into the holy of holies- the place wherein there is no darkness- wherein he shall find peace.

So be it he shall earn his own passport- he shall qualify for his passport- and I say he shall not be denied admittance when he has so qualified himself.

Now let it be understood that I judge not- for I am not the judge- I am The Wayshower- and I come that ye might know the way- and for this do I give unto thee the law- in its essence - in its simplicity- I say the law is exacting- and perfect in its action- it is a law of balance and harmony- all nature strives to bring about balance in the world of form- be ye as one with it- work with it- resist not the law of truth and justice which is harmony- for this do I speak unto thee thusly- be ye at peace and rest in the knowing that-

I am the Lord thy God--

Sananda

Recorded by Sister Thedra

Self-Application of The Law

Beloved ones- the way is made clear and it is now prepared, the place for thee- I say the place is prepared for thee- and ye shall be put therein- and therein ye shall be in thine own environment- while it is within thine own power to choose thine environment- I say unto thee, prepare thineself for the <u>highest</u>- for the lightest- and be ye as ones responsible for thine own preparation-

Now it is said, that when one hast prepared himself he shall be put into the holy of holies- within the inner temple- yet none enter therein me unprepared- I am The Wayshower- I am He which hast gone before thee to prepare the way-

Now I say unto thee it is thine part to live the law, apply it as it is given unto thee, and the law is simply given; and for this has it been given as thou hast been able to comprehend it- for it is not complicated, it is given in its simplicity and for this have I given it unto thee in this manner that the child might comprehend it- waver not in the application of the law- and give unto no man the bitter cup- for I say unto thee: ye drink of thine own cup- let it be sweet- for this do I speak thusly- I come that ye might have the law, that ye might know, that where I go ye might go also-

Now I say unto thee: look unto thine own part, thine own actions, thine own sowing and let thine brothers actions speak for themself- and let him be his own peacemaker- <u>that is</u>, let him find his own house clean, and establish peace within his own heart- yet, ye shall give unto him the "word"- and let it suffice that ye have eaten* thereof and found it good-

Now ye shall make no mockery of the "word"- be ye not a hypocrite for I say woe unto the <u>hypocrite.</u>

I am not deceived-

Let thine own light so shine that all might see it from afar- let thine own place be as ye have made it, and none shall deprive thee of thine own creation- that which thou hast created for thine self- so be it that I have spoken simply and frankly that all might be prepared-

I say unto thee be ye as ones prepared for the greater part- for this do I speak-

I Am Sananda

* applied the law and found that it works.

Recorded by Sister Thedra

To the Ones Which Seek High Places of Honor – Ethics

Thine hand shall be Mine hand, and ye shall give unto them this word, and it shall be for the good of all-

I say- "<u>it shall be for the good of all</u>" This day it is said that the ones which seek high places of honor, shall themself be honorable and trustworthy- they shall be obedient unto the law- the law which I bring- they shall be ethical in all their dealings- and they shall not deceive themself- for I say- therein is the greatest of folly-

They shall abide by the law of God- by the law of the land wherein they abide- they shall be as ones honest with themself- and they shall <u>know</u> that which they do is in keeping with the law- and they shall be fresh of spirit- they shall be as ones prepared for great inspiration- and they shall receive the word of God- and be humble of spirit- and for this shall they be i<u>n</u>spired- for I say unto them the servants of God walk softly in the presence of the Lord- they flaunt not themself before their fellow men- neither do they betray their trust nor their fellow men-

Now I say, it is come when great responsibility shall rest upon their shoulders- for there shall be much confusion- much suffering and great stress- yet there are ones which have come into the Earth to assist at this time- that the darkness might be dispelled-

And great shall be their part- yet I say it is given unto each to have a part- and blest is he which finds himself prepared for the <u>greater</u> part- for this do I say unto them: hear ye Mine words, and harken unto them for they shall stand thee in good stead-

For I am come that there be light-

So be it I am the Lord thy God

Sananda

Recorded by Sister Thedra

To Them Which Seek Places of Honor in High Places
To the People

Wherein is it said that there are none so sad as the ones which betray themself - I say unto thee there are none so sad as the one which betrays himself or his trust-

Now ye shall be unto them Mine hand and Mine voice and give unto them this word- and they shall remember it - for I say unto them which seek places of honor in high places they shall be mindful of their own responsibility- they shall be unto themself true- they shall serve selflessly- and with joy- while I say there shall be great stress and unrest amongst the people- I say for a surety that it is given unto some to come into embodiment at this time to give of themself that this day bring forth an abundance of fruit such as hast not been known before- and these shall be a lamp unto the feet of their fellow man- they shall sacrifice themself for the good of all- these shall be as the ones sent that the Earth be lifted up- that there be light-

I say these which serve selflessly are the ones which have come into bodies of mortal flesh that the Earth be prepared for Her new part- and for this have I been unto them Sibor and I have seen them as ones preparing themself for this part which they now play- and play it well they shall--

I say they have volunteered for the part which they now have taken upon themself, and they shall not be forgotten- for a host stands by to give assistance where it is wise and prudent-.

I say we trespass not upon their free will- until it is given unto us of the Father and for the good of all- for we shall not stand by and see Mine people sacrificed unto the dragon- I say we shall not permit Mine people to be given the bitter cup- for it is finished and done- this age shall be as one new- a new order- a new day- and it shall bring forth great light. So be it and Selah-

I Am the Lord thy God

Sananda

Recorded by Sister Thedra

To the People - Mine Flock

This day I would say unto them, there are but few which are mindful of their trust- their great responsibility which is placed upon them-. The ones which have put their trust in the ones which sit in high places have given unto them "super power"-credit for being trustworthy- and there are many- too many which have betrayed themself and their trust-

Yet I say unto the people- be ye as ones responsible for thine own part- for thine own role within this drama upon this stage, whereupon thou art playing the game of life- betray not thine ownself- for therein is the greatest of folly- I say ye shall do thine own part- and be ye self-responsible- shift not thine responsibility unto another- give no man credit for being thine "Master- thine Savior", or responsible for thine salvation! I say ye, each one, is responsible for thine own <u>actions</u>, thine own misused energy- and the transmuting of it-

I say, that when it comes that ye have finished thine days upon the Earth ye shall be faced with that which ye have done- and ye shall know wherein ye have failed or betrayed thineself- ye shall have the opportunity to begin again, and to correct it- Yet I say why wait ye? this is the day of salvation- this is the day for which thou hast waited-

Now ye shall be as ones prepared for the next part- and it behooves thee to give credit where credit is due- and ye shall be as ones blest-

Ye shall make no mockery of the law- ye shall be as ones honest with thineself and give unto thineself credit for being the greatest of the great- ye shall not give any man dominion over thee- ye shall be as his equal- ye shall be as his servant- as his brother, as his child, as his parent- ye shall not be his superior, for I say there are none greater, none lesser- for art thou not of one parent born?- of one Eternal parent thou art born--

Now I say unto thee thou shall be as brothers all- as the ones gone forth, that ye might glorify the Father upon the Earth- and be ye as sons of God- walk ye becomingly- and let thine light so shine- be ye as ones which have thine hand in Mine and I shall direct thee, I shall lead thee, for this have I revealed Mineself unto thee- Now ye shall be as ones prepared to go where I go, and none enter into the place of Mine abode unprepared- while it is given unto Me to be the Lord thy God- I say unto thee thou art the ones which I come to find- which I come to gather out- that ye might return unto Mine Father with Me-

Now, I say unto thee- none other shall hear Mine words, Mine voice, for their ears shall be stopped, their eyes blinded- and they shall deny Me- and these shall not be given* as Mine flock: for Mine flock shall know Mine voice and answer Me- I shall know Mine flock by their light- for is their light not Mine? And do I not know Mine own? I say unto thee thou shall be no part of their willfulness- for it is not becoming unto Mine flock- while I say unto thee many sleepeth yet- and it is given unto them to be as ones dreaming dreams which doth disturb them- and for this shall they awaken, and arise, and come alive- I say they shall be as ones come alive- and they shall walk with Me, and talk with Me, and know as I know; so shall it be a glad day-

I am He which is sent that it be so-

I Am Sananda

Son of God the Father

Solen Aum Solen

* They shall not receive as...

To the Servants of the Lord and the Laggards

Wherein is it said that there would be great stress upon the people- and is it not so? I say unto thee it is so: and for this do I speak this day- I speak unto them which are of a mind to follow Me, to serve with Me

now that the great plan be brought forth, that there be light in the world of men- so let it be understood that the ones which choose to follow Me shall be as ones prepared to serve me and the plan, These shall serve selflessly and <u>fearlessly</u>- these shall be favored, for I shall give unto them great strength- and wisdom for there shall be need for such as I have for them-- while I say the ones which are rebellious and unworthy shall not receive- and the traitors shall be disarmed- while I know the fullness of the plan they know not, yet I shall reveal many things unto Mine servants, Mine prophets, Mine flock which serve me diligently-

Now I say unto these which have given of themself that there be light, that the plan be fulfilled- bring thine whole self - thine whole heart unto the Father as thine sacrifice- for none other can he use- thine hands shall be His, thine feet shall be His, and ye shall be as the living example of His manifestation- for He hast given of Himself that ye might be- so be ye as one which knows--

While I say unto the ones which go in and out of places of <u>so-called "worship"</u>- ye shall be as ones prepared for a great awakening- for thine preconceived ideas shall be as nought- for it is now come when ye shall <u>know</u> and know that ye <u>know</u>! for long hast thou spoken of Me as one responsible for thine misused energy- yet this day I say unto thee: ye are responsible for thine every <u>act</u>, for thine <u>own</u> <u>salvation.</u> Throw off thine lethargy, cut away thine leg irons and arise ye and know that I am come, that where I go ye might go also. Be ye not of a mind to wait for I say the time is come when I shall gather Mine own out from amongst the laggards and I shall put them in the place which is prepared for them and I shall go unto Mine Father and the door shall again be closed for a season- and these which wait shall wait for another season in yet another place- another time. I say: Oh, ye laggards, pity shall be the ones which wait- arise, come forth and follow Me- for I am the Lord thy God.

Sananda

Recorded by Sister Thedra

Rescue from the Oppressor

Mine children- ye shall partake of Mine banquet table- ye shall feast, and be filled to capacity, ye shall be satisfied, and no more shall ye hunger- I say: <u>NO MORE</u> shall ye hunger for I shall satisfy thine hunger- and thine longing shall be no more- I say unto thee: thine longing shall be satisfied and no more shall ye go into bondage- darkness-.

Mine children, I have sent Mine emissaries unto thee; without number have they come- and they have been oppressed, and they have been martyred for thine sake, for the love which they bore- yet I say, it is now time that they be finished, that they be brought out from amongst the oppressors- and no longer shall they bear the burdens of the laggards- the oppressors- I say they shall complete their mission and return unto their abiding place wherein they shall be free from all bondage- wherein they shall know no sorrow or oppression- I say, them which have given their all selflessly shall partake of Mine board- and they shall have no wants, no fear, no sorrow- So shall it be a glad day when they return unto Me- unscathed, unharmed, purified, and justified-

TO THE OPPRESSOR:

I speak unto them which know not that this day is come when I shall bring out Mine "flock" from among the multitude which hast oppressed them- be ye alert, and know that the law of justice shall reign supreme- and there shall be justice for all- according unto his works- I say ye shall be judged with <u>righteous</u> <u>judgment-</u> and it shall be meted out according to the law of justice which is exacting.

Be ye not so foolish as to <u>think</u> ye escape the law- I say ye shall be unto thine own self true and unto thine trust true- be ye mindful of Mine words- and Mine servants which I have sent that ye might have light- I say ye shall be blest according unto thine works- and ye shall bless others as ye would be blest- I speak out this day that ye might come to know that <u>I</u> <u>am</u> <u>come</u>- come that there be light- so let it be-

I Am the Lord thy God

Sananda

Recorded by Sister Thedra

Sori Sori
From Glory to Glory - From Galaxy to Galaxy

Sori Sori, while it is given unto thee to walk in flesh, thou art not bound by flesh- for I say unto thee thou art <u>spirit</u>- <u>of</u> <u>spirit</u> born, thou art <u>not</u> <u>of</u> <u>flesh</u>: thou art <u>not</u> of Earth- for I say unto thee thou art of spirit-

Thou comest into the place wherein thou art with the will which is thine: thine own will which hast been unto thee of the Father in the beginning- and there is a time, and a place- unto all manifestation- and when the time is come each manifestation shall be completed, and it shall run its courses* and be as the illusion which it is- for spirit shall withdraw from its manifestation and be spirit still, no less for its manifestation, no less for releasing its manifestation, and greater for the expression in manifestation- I say it is now come when many forms shall change- and greater shall be the manifestation- more brilliant- more glorious manifestation! I say- ye go from glory unto glory- from galaxy unto galaxy- such is perfection on each; I have spoken and I am that I am-

Sori Sori

*cycle

Recorded by Sister Thedra

Thou Art Mine Children

Solen Aum Solen

Beloved ones, Mine hand is not shortened, Mine strength is not diminished- Mine time is not lessened- and I am come that Mine work be done on the Earth in this day- this age- for this new day- this new dispensation shall bring forth such harvest as the world hast not known- I say such harvest as this age shall bring forth the Earth hast not known- so be it that I have sent forth great and mighty ones that there be great light- I shall bring forth that which mortal mind hast not as yet conceived- for I shall do a strange and mighty work through them as Mine hands and Mine feet- for these are Mine servants which shall serve as Mine hands and feet upon the Earth-

Now I say unto thee: be ye as ones blest to be among these which I have sent- for I say, great and mighty things shall ye do- and thou hast as yet not seen the fullness of thine labors for thine labors shall yield up a mighty harvest, and ye shall reap and be glad ye shall be partakers of Mine harvest- for I shall be mindful of thee- and I shall not forsake thee- be ye joyful in the days of thine labors and sing ye a glad song; let thine heart sing for joy! for I tell thee of a surety thou art <u>Mine children</u> which I have sent forth to do a great and mighty work-

Be ye as one prepared for the greater part- waste not thine time on the laggards for these shall have their day- their place- and weary not of Mine work- love ye one another- rejoice in Mine work- and return unto Me - for this do I send Mine Son that ye might return unto Me with Him-

I am thine Father

Solen Aum Solen

Recorded by Sister Thedra

I Didst Image Thee Perfect

Solen Aum Solen

By Mine hand shall ye be sustained- by Mine grace shall ye be kept- I Say: "by Mine grace shall ye be kept". and it is because of Mine love for <u>Mine</u> <u>children</u> that I extend Mine hand- that I enfold thee within Mine bosom- I am thine Father Eternal- for I have given unto thee of Mineself that ye might have thine being- and for this thou art eternal beings- within Me <u>thou art,</u> and because of Me thou art- and no man shall be given his inheritance in full without Me-- for from Me there is nought- for I am the fullness of thine existence- all that man shall <u>become</u> <u>I</u> <u>AM</u>- and because I Am. I say unto thee, all I have is thine and ye have but to claim it, and deny it not, for it hast not as yet been revealed unto thee that which ye shall become- for I say unto thee, ye go from glory unto glory- and ye become the sons of God- that which thou wast born to be- I say thou wast created in Mine <u>image</u>- for <u>I</u> <u>didst</u> <u>image</u> <u>thee</u> <u>perfect</u> in the beginning and thou shall return unto Me perfect- as thou went forth from Me- so be it I have willed it so- So let it be-

I Am thine Father

Solen Aum Solen

Thine Abiding Place - Thine Return -Thine Inheritance

Mine children while it is not yet time to return unto thine abiding place- I say unto thee, "be ye as ones prepared", for the day approaches when ye shall be as the ones returned, I say ye <u>shall</u> return and <u>so</u> <u>great</u> shall be thine joy that all the cosmos shall reverberate the glad songs-

While it is but the lesser part which thou now have, I say ye shall receive the greater part- ye shall return unto thine abiding place and ye shall know no pain, no longing, all thine longings shall be fulfilled and ye shall be forever at peace-. I say, ye shall rest in Me knowing thine source and rejoicing in the knowing- be ye at peace- and be ye glad <u>this</u> day is come when I speak unto thee of thine sonship- and so great shall be thine inheritance! ye shall be as ones returned unto thine place of abode and therein ye shall find thine inheritance which I have willed unto thee from the beginning- so be it that-

I AM thine Father Eternal

Solen Aum Solen

Recorded by Thedra

The Cry Goes Out - Awaken!!

Ye shall be unto the Father His children, for nothing shall separate thee from Him- thou art separate from Him only because of thine illusions, thine thinking, thine dreams which thou hast dreamed- I say: now thine illusions, thine dreams shall end- and ye shall know thine self to be one with Him, the Father which hast given unto thee being- so be it that I come that it be so- so let it be--

I tell thee of a surety, thou art of divine origin- perfect in thine own right- 'Sons of God art thou'- and ye shall remember that which I say unto thee- let not thine illusions dim thine sight- I have said that ye shall be prepared for the greater part- for this have I come- let thine eyes be opened, thine ears be made to hear- yet ye shall be of a mind to hear- I say rid thineself of all thine puny ways, thine opinions of and about Me- and be ye of a mind to learn: hear ye that which I say unto thee, cast away thine leg irons which hast bound thee- I say, free thineself of all thine preconceived ideas of Me and about Me, for I come unto thee in this day in ways ye know not of, for I have come- I am come- fear not that I am come, for I come that ye be gathered in- let no man tell thee it is not so! For I tell thee of a surety that it is so-

Now ye shall bless thineself to keep thine own counsel, ask no man his opinions - for I say unto thee this is the puny part of wisdom- for they but serve to hold thee bound- let no man bind thee by his opinions- and I have said: "I shall come as a thief in the night- the hour no man knoweth"- so it is: and I say unto thee: A mighty work I shall do while the sleepers sleep on- so be it they shall awaken and find that I have come and gone- and they knew not! Be ye up and about the Father's business- and follow ye Me-- I say: be ye about the Father's business!-

Awaken! ye that sleep! come forth! and follow ye Me!

For this is no time to sleep!

I bid thee arise, shake off thine legirons, hasten ye- and be ye alert- for this do I cry out AWAKEN!!

I Am the Lord thy God

Sananda

Recorded by Sister Thedra

Keep Watch

For this day I would give unto thee this word, know that which I say unto thee- for it is for their benefit that I give it unto thee- let them which have a mind to learn hear that which I have said: let them take it unto themself as their own, for it shall profit them.

I say: it is the law that ye love one another that ye be unto each other mindful- that ye bless thine self in so doing- no hatred shall be within thee for thine brother- neither any creature which doth crawl, creep, run, or fly upon the Earth- for hatred shall be put from thee- I say ye shall not partake of that which the forces of darkness do- yet ye shall pity them for their unknowing- and let them be: for love overcomes all darkness- I say love <u>them</u>, give not of thine time or energy resisting them- yet ye shall not relax thine watch- for ye shall work diligently and pray without ceasing that the Father's will be done upon the Earth as it is in the realms of light- I say ye shall be mindful of <u>thine</u> <u>own</u> part, and be ye not divided- for when ye give unto the forces of darkness credit for disturbing thine peace they have gained a victory over thee and I say unto thee: "be ye at peace" and let no man take it from thee, for it is thine inheritance, and ye have but to claim it now!!

While I say, be ye no part of their foolishness- I say, it behooves thee to keep thine mind, thine heart set on that which hast been given unto thee, that which hast been given from the source of light- and that which is given unto thee to do- let not their works deceive thee, or be unto thee a trap- for it is given unto them, the forces of darkness, to trip thee up, and for this do I say, "relax not thine watch" while I see them working without ceasing that they might weave their nefarious web, I say unto thee, be ye at peace, cling unto the law of love, peace and justice- and <u>know</u> ye that I am come that there be light, so let it be-

I Am that I Am

Sananda

Recorded by Sister Thedra

The Oil in the Lamp

By Mine own hand have I blest thee; and by the word have I blest thee: with Mine presence have I blest thee: and I say unto thee, let all which come within thine presence be blest of thee and by thee, and for thine presence let them be blest- for I say it is thine part to bless others as I bless thee- let it be so-

Say unto them that the time is now come when they shall be as ones prepared to give unto others in like manner- for I say unto them, there are many which do walk within their midst prepared to administer unto them, yet it is given unto Me to see them preparing the bitter cup for their neighbor- for their brother- I say unto them: let thine own cup be sweetened- for ye shall drink the cup which thou hast prepared for him- while ye put forth thine hand that he be blest thou dost receive Mine blessing- for this do I speak unto thee: receive of Me as thou givest unto him- for I say unto thee "as ye give so do ye receive"- let it be sweet.

Now it is said, that, ye are found by thine own light- so let it shine, and love is the oil which burns brightly- so keep thine own lamp trimmed and burning- I come that there be light- So let it be-

I am the Lord thy God

Sananda

No Greater Love - Than Sibor for Sibet

Behold the word made manifest! Behold the power of the word, for I say unto thee the power of the word shall be made manifest before thee-

I say, the power of the "WORD" shall be made manifest before thee! and ye shall behold it- ye shall work with the <u>word</u>- and know the power thereof- for this have I Sibored thee- for this do I speak unto thee this day- that ye might become the Sons of God <u>Illumined</u> - and that ye might be Sibors unto others yet in darkness;

For I say unto thee, the time is nigh when thine greater part shall become apparent- and ye shall accept the great responsibility which it carries- for therein is no greater responsibility than that of Sibor for His Sibets, no greater love than Sibor for His Sibets, and for this do We labor without ceasing or reward- other than thine own illumination, so be it I am thine Sibor, thine Brother.

Sanat Kumara

Recorded by Sister Thedra

**Unto Them Which Seek Light
Of Death**

This day I would say unto them which seek light, that this day is the day which is given unto them- none other do they have, this is the day of salvation- this is the day of gladness- this is the day of joy- this is the day for which thou hast waited-

Now I say arise! Accept thine inheritance and be ye glad that it is given unto thee to be a 'Son of God'-

While many shall leave their Earthly vehicles and go into yet other realms - I say they shall not be aware of their sonship, or their identity, their divinity- while others shall lay aside the garment of flesh and step forth into their garment body of light substance knowing themself to be 'Sons of God'- they shall not die- they shall be as ones free forevermore- Now let it be understood that death is not the severance of flesh bonds, for ne're was it so.

I say, death is not the severance of the bonds of flesh- for flesh is but the vehicle used for a time and discarded for yet grander, more glorious forms of light substance - so be ye as ones prepared- I say ye shall not fear the change which has been called <u>death</u> which is <u>not</u> death. For this is but part of thine unknowing- thine illusion- thine dreams-

FEAR NOT!

I am speaking unto them which have a mind to learn- ears to hear- and a will to return unto their rightful estate-

So be it I am the Lord thy God

Sananda

Recorded by Sister Thedra

The Power of the Word

Say unto them which ask of thee that the time is now come when they shall put on the whole armor of God and they shall make no mockery of the word, for I say unto them the word is holy- and powerful- it is the power of the word which sustains them within the world of form-for the word is made manifest before them- either for weal or woe- I say the word sustains their world of form- for the word is made manifest and they know it not!

I say unto them misuse not the power of the word- and be ye mindful of thine words, for they shall return unto thee bearing their likeness- let it be becoming unto thee- let it be sweet- be ye aware of the power of the word- for great is the power thereof- Now while it is yet time, let no word pass from thine lips of hatred, malice or of deceit- for it shall return unto thee as the bitter cup and ye shall drink thereof- so be it the law- I am come that ye know the law- so be it: it is given unto thee simply and clearly-

I Am the Son of God

Sananda

Recorded by Sister Thedra of the Emerald Cross

Mission Statement

Give the truth to the world. Let it be received where it will. Many will read the messages. Some will accept the truth, others will read through curiosity, a few will ridicule. Yet to all is the truth given, and to all remains the power of choice.

The hope of the world in these times is in spiritualizing all forms of activity---promoting understanding through love and service. These must be the watchwords if the world is to come into lasting peace. We are trying to influence a world that is going astray and could cause undreamed of suffering. We are trying to overcome the thought of materialists and to bring a spiritual outlook into the earthly life. We need the help of all on earth who can think in spiritual terms. The great battle to be fought now is between the spiritual and the material, between idealism and carnalism. You can help by spreading the word---we are asking that you help because the battle may be long and the victory far away.

Halls of Light is not allied with any sect, denomination, political entity, organization, neither endorses nor opposes any cause. There are no dues for membership. Halls of Light is self-supporting through its own voluntary contributions. Halls of Light has but one purpose: to help through encouragement and understanding...

To contact the publishers or to obtain copies of our other books, please contact us at email: goldtown11@gmail.com

Sananda's Appearance

Be ye as one which hast heard Mine Voice and responded unto it - for I speak that ye hear, and I say that which is wise and prudent.

Let it be known that 1, the Lord thy God hast spoken and bear ye witness of Me, for I have made manifest Mineself that ye might know Me - and for this wast these manifestations made.

I say that I have made Mineself manifest that ye might see Me with thine mortal eyes; that ye might bear witness of Me. Yet thine companions saw and believed not; neither did they hear, for they were selfish and unprepared - yet, did I deny them?

I say; I came that they which would might see and hear. I went and came again unto Mine own. So be it that I have found; I have given unto the found that they which know not might know; that they might come to know as thou knowest.

Yet, how many hast turned from Me and persecuted thee for Mine Word. It is said, "Woe unto them which persecute Mine servants." is it not the law which they set into motion?

Yea Mine beloved, I say they bring about their own downfall. So be it that I am a compassionate one, and I would that they know what they do. So be it they shall learn well their lessons. So let it be, for this is the mercy of God, the One which hast sent Me.

So be it. I AM The Wayshower, the Lord thy God

I AM Sananda

About the Late Sister Thedra

Since the later part of the last Century, the *Kumara* wisdom has begun to reemerge into the world. This process began with the late Sister Thedra, whom Jesus Christ appeared physically to while on her deathbed and spontaneously healed her of cancer while she was in the Yucatan, where she had gone to accept her fate and the will of our Lord Jesus Christ.

That is when something miraculous occurred. Jesus spoke to her saying, "My name is Esu Sananda Kumara" and then sent Thedra down to the Monastery of the Seven Rays in Peru to learn the Kumara wisdom. After five years, Thedra was told to return to the United States where she founded the Association of Sananda and Sanat Kumara at Mt. Shasta in California.

While heading this organization, Thedra channeled many messages from Sananda and taught the Kumara wisdom until her passing in 1992. While in the Yucatan, it is said that Sister Thedra, during the 1960s, was associated with the Kumara.

Sister Thedra, 1900-1992, spent five years at an abbey undergoing intensive spiritual training and initiations. While in South America, she had an experience which changed her in an instant when, as it is told by her, Jesus Christ physically appeared to her and spontaneously cured her of cancer.

He introduced himself to her by his true, name, "Sananda Kumara," thereby revealing his affiliation with the founders of the

Great Solar Brotherhoods. It was by His command that Sister Thedra went to Peru. She eventually left upon being told that her experience there was complete. She then traveled to Mt. Shasta in California and founded the Association of Sananda and Sanat Kumara. A.S.S.K.

You ask, Is There a difference between Jesus and Sananda? Our Lord's name given at birth by his Father Joseph and his beloved mother Mary was Yeshua, thus being of the house of David and the order of Yoseph he would be called Yeshua ben Yoseph. The Roman Emperors placed the name of Jesus upon the sir-name of Yeshua after the Emperor Justinian adopted Christianity as the official faith of Rome and ordered that the sacred books be compiled upon approval of a specially appointed counsel appointed by the Emperor into a recognizable and uniform work titled "The Bible". Prior to this, there never was a Bible per se.

There existed until the time of the Emperor's edict, a selection of many Sacred texts, that were employed in the Sacred Teachings, many of which were copies of what the Greeks had transposed from the original texts in the Libraries of Alexandria, which were originally compiled by Alexander the Great, and were destroyed by Julius Caesar who feared that they might prove dangerous to the rule of a Caesar, an Earthly God.

In addition, it was to keep the knowledge of Alexander's Libraries out of the hands of the Ptolemy's who were said to be descended from his bloodline. (At the time, Caesar had no way of knowing that vast portions of the Library were already in the

Americas, in the Great Universities of the Inca, and in possession of the Mayans.)

Yeshua spent many years in the East after his ascension. The Good Shepherd, upon his appearances to the Apostles after His ascension, told them that He was going to tend to His Father's other sheep; which meant, plainly, that He was continuing upon His sacred journey. As The Ascended One, Yeshua took to Himself the name of Sananda, meaning the Christed One, and Sananda was thus embraced forevermore by the Great Solar Brotherhood. To many of you. this is all new. To others it will be received as a welcome easing of the wall that has so long separated two sides of the same coin. This knowledge is being placed into the ethers and the matrix of thought at this time as it is the time of The Great Awakening and the Christos is already emerging into the new consciousness.

Authority to use the name of Sananda was given to Sister Thedra when Jesus, (Sananda) appeared to her in the Yucatan and cured her instantly of the cancer that had taken over her body. Further, He allowed a picture of his countenance (included herein) to be taken at that time that she might realize the occurrence was more than a dream.

Sanada's Message to her by Sister Thedra: "Sori Sori: Mine hand I have placed upon thine head, and I have given unto thee the authority to use Mine name. Give unto them the name Sananda, by which they shall know Me as the Lord thy God - the Son of God, sent that ye be made to know me, the One sent from out The Inner Temple that there be Light in the world of men. Now it is come when ones which have the will to follow Me shall come to know Me by that name which I commanded thee to give unto the world as Mine New name.

There are many that shall call upon the name of Jesus, yet they will deny the new name as they are want to do. Unto thee I give assurance that I am the One sent that there be Light in the world of men. Now let this be understood, that they that deny Mine New Name, deny Me by any name. So be it I have appointed thee Mine spokesman; I've given unto thee the power and authority to speak for being that which I AM. And I say unto thee Mine child whom I have called forth and anointed thee with the Holy Spirit, thy name shall be as it is now called, Thedra, that name I spoke unto thee from out the ethers, and thou heard Me and accepted that which I gave unto thee; and wherein have I deceived thee? Wherein have I forgotten thee, or left thee alone?"

I say unto thee: "Mine hand is upon thee and I shall sustain thee and you shall come to know that which I have kept for thee. So be it that I have kept thy reward, and at no time shall it be dissipated or scattered, for it is intact. So let this Mine Word suffice them which question thee - let them question, and I shall bear witness for thee. For do I not know Mine servants from the traitors? Do I not reward Mine servants according unto their works or merits? I speak that they might know that I am mindful of Mine servants, that I am not a poor puny priest who has forgotten his servants.

"I say unto them, Mine servants shall be glorified above the crowned heads of the nations which have set themselves apart, and denied Me Mine part of Mine word for they have turned from Me in their conceit and forgetfulness. Now let this go on record as Mine

Word, and I shall give unto them proof, which are of a mind to follow Me. So be it as I have spoken and I am not finished; I shall speak again and again, and I shall rise Mine Voice against them which set foot against Mine servants, and they shall be as ones cast out. So let them ask of Me and I shall enlighten them. So be it I know where of I speak. Be ye as ones blest to accept Me and know Me for that which I AM."

On Saturday, June 13, 1992, at exactly 10.00 PM, at the age of 92, Sister Thedra made her final transition from the comfort of her own bed. When the time arrived, she simply took one small breath and slipped quietly away, without pomp or fanfare.

She left as she had lived: as a humble servant for the greater good. The messages included were given to Sister Thedra before her transition. They are compiled here to give you some idea of the significance of her passing and of the expansion of the work, as she is now free to work unencumbered by the physical limitations and by the pain which has so encumbered her in the past. She has carried on the work here on the Earth plane for the last 50 years because that is where the work was needed. Rest assured that her work now in the higher realms will simply be an extension of that work.

Divine Explanations

Part - I

The following explanations and definitions of terms used by Sananda (Jesus) and the various Sibors were given by Sananda through direct revelation. They are not alphabetical. These explanations should be read over and over.

- - - - - - - - - - -

"My Beloved Sibors please give us plainly the definitions of the following words that there may be no error on our part." - Thedra.

THEMSELF? What is the explanation of your terminology of "Themself" – "themselves"?

"I (Sananda) say unto thee mine beloved, they which would be unto thee a vessel, unto thee a sibor, unto thee teacher, are as ones enlightened of the Father, enlightened of the Father for the light is in them.

They know their parts well, they have their memory, they have mastered the elements, they can do all the things which I do and they take unto "themself" no credit for they have overcome self. They are self-less. Now I say unto them: them which work with thee are the Selfless ones. They ask <u>nothing</u> for "themself." Now while this is true they are as one.

They are within the great brotherhood of the Selfless Ones - the Ones clothed in white. They are as the Royal Assembly - and each unto his own, yet each for all and all for one. Now while in thy world, they (of thy world) are <u>selfish</u> and they are not for the whole - they ask for self and I speak of these as the selfish ones. I speak unto them in terms which they shall come to know and therein is wisdom.

I say that they shall be responsible for "themself" and as a world of me I say they shall be responsible for their society; they "themself" have created it. Now I speak unto thee mine beloved, I say "ye shall be responsible for thyself. He shall be responsible for himself. They as a whole shall be responsible for that which they have created, while thou art responsible unto thyself for thine part - and not held accountable for theirs. Be it so."

BELEIS? "Mighty is the word and great the power thereof. I say unto thee this word carries with it the part of surrender. The word is the release of power - that which is sent forth by the one which asks of the Father His blessing. It is the surrender of the self - the complete surrender of the personal will and letting the Father's will be accomplished in all things through thee. "<u>So</u> <u>be</u> <u>it</u>" - it the accomplishment, the acceptance of the Father's plan."

SELAH? - "The word carries the Seal of Truth - meaning it is without error - no mistake - it is the verification of Truth - not subject to change.

SIBET? – "The Sibet is one which has offered or presented himself as a candidate for the greater learning and for the greater initiation. He comes as an empty vessel that he may be filled. So be it."

SIBOR? - "I am the Sibor of Sibors." - "The Sibor is one which has been illumined of God the Father. He has returned unto the Father purified. He has gone the Royal Road - which means he has overcome death. He has mastered the lower elements - he controls the elements. He can raise the dead - heal the sick - he can create like unto the Father for he has finished his course and won the victory and returned unto the Father the Victor. So be it."

"I am the Sibor of Sibors. I am the first born of Him which hast sent me. Sananda."

LEGIRONS? - "Beloved - I say unto thee: thy opinions and thy dogmas are not the least of these - neither thy creeds. Be it ever that these are great and heavy ones. Now let it be understood that a leg-iron is something which holds thee bound. It is something which holds thee, it keeps thee fast, wherein progress is not possible. Now that progress be made possible, ye shall cut away the legirons.

Knowest thou these bound by legirons? These are to be pitied, they drag them with them, impeding their progress - and they are as ones bound! They are not free - are they? While they serve their sentence - they are as ones bound - they are bond-men - they are bound men - men bound. Now let me say I too am a "bondsman." I came that they may be free. I say I bring unto thee the law which thou shall obey - unto the letter - then I shall give unto thee that which I have kept for thee. Be ye as one prepared for that.

PREPARATION? Now - preparation - what do you mean by "preparation?" "This my beloved is the part which they shall do - the part of preparation is: cleaning thyself of all the opinions, indoctrinations of man. The cup must be emptied. This is thy part, the becoming the '"little child" unopinionated, unscathed and unmarred with or by their doctrines, creeds and crafts. I say the child is unindoctrinated and un-opinonated and is the virgin mind – (yet it does not remain so long in this world). While the little child represents the empty cup - the empty vessel, the Virgin Spirit, it is given unto the child to be one which has come from other realms and to have been in many embodiments, many times: yet the symbol of virginity. Wherein is it said there are none innocent among thee?

WHEREIN I AM? - "Now while thou art yet within the world of men - I am within mine Father's realm, the place wherein there is no darkness, wherein <u>ALL</u> things are known. I say wherein <u>ALL</u> things are known, wherein there is <u>No</u> mystery.

And too - I say when thou hast attained unto thy Royal Road, when thou hast become part of the Royal Assembly, thou shall know as I - thou shall be as I - thou shall be brought into the place wherein I am, for I say unto thee this is attainment. This is the day of Attainment, the day of "becoming," the day of thy salvation. Know ye that this is Mine day - the day for which thou hast waited? I say unto thee: "This is the day of fulfillment. This is Mine Day. Mine Day is come ---"

What is meant by "ALL THE LANDS OF THE EARTH?"- "This I mean, all the lands of the Earth. I have said it, I mean it as I have said it and there is no mystery of or to it."

ALL MANKIND? "This is Mine people - Mine children - Mine flock - Mine Church - Mine brethren - Mine congregation unto whom I shall minister. By Mine own hand shall they be fed and led. These have I came to find. Are not all <u>hu</u>-man beings considered "Man kind"? by thine own standards. Yet all men are not of me."

WHAT DO YOU MEAN - "WILL IT SO"? - "There is power in the "WILL" and the power which they use to create their own torment and confusion is misused energy. Yet they will this - they will it so. Now when ye will to serve me ye give unto me thy undivided attention, the whole heart - thy heart - thine ALL. Yet I say that they which doth attempt to serve me with one hand and the dragon with the other has not willed to serve me. They are not of me - they are not of Mine flock. I say they are either with me or against me. I cannot accept the one hand while they reserve the other for the dragon. They are not wholeheartedly mine.

I make no compromises with the dragon. Mine shall come out from them and surrender unto me themself - their all - without reservation. This is willing it so - for they will the Father's will be done in them, through them, by them. They leave no energy that the dragon may use. They use all their energy to serve me. This is mine word unto thee."

WHAT IS DARKNESS? - "Thine Un-Knowing - thy darkness comes from the fall of man - which one was with God the Father perfect which didst have his memory blanked from him when he didst transgress."

MAYAS VEIL? - "The result of such unknowing - the darkness which man has brought upon himself. The part he has created for himself."

WHAT DOES IT MEAN TO <u>BETRAY ONES SELF</u>? - "This is the sad part for first the 'fall' came from his betrayal - and it hast resulted in the fall - in the veil of Maya - the "illusion" and in thy un-knowing - in thy own darkness."

WHAT OF BETRAYING "HIS OWN TRUST"? - "The plan is all inclusive and includes <u>all</u> - yet there are ones unaware of the "plan" - (and they are not as included in this temple as yet) - no personal reference unto the ones within this temple. Now when one becomes aware of his part, he is given the law and it is provided for his own good - and he has the law clearly stated, plainly recorded, and he turns his face away - that he may hide from it. He puts his fingers into his ears that he may not hear it. He gives unto his benefactors the bitter cup and he goes his own willful way.

He has betrayed himself for he shall be caught up short of his course. When he has been given a chance - a "part" within the plan and he has committed himself, he has the responsibility given unto him for that "part" and should he be so foolish as to betray his trust he shall be like unto one which has thrown overboard his <u>own</u> life belt - poor foolish ones!"

WISDOM? - What is meant by the word "Wisdom?" - "Wisdom is that which is light, the knowledge of the law and its proper use. The right use of the law - and this Mine children is Mine part. I come that ye may BECOME wise! Wisdom is thy divine gift - not of man, for man of Earth is foolish indeed - and he is nothing save that which the Father has endowed him. All else is of the world of "illusion" which shall pass into nothingness in the Light which I Am."

WHAT IS THE "PEARL OF GREAT PRICE, THE PRICELESS PEARL? - "That which I offer thee - thy freedom, thy salvation from bondage - thine inheritance in full - Mine word which is not purchased with coin - not bought, neither is it sold. It is the wisdom of which I speak. Mine offer unto thee is without price - it is the 'pearl' - "Mine Pearl."

WHY ARE MIS-SPELLED AND GRAMMATICAL ERRORS USED IN THESE SCRIPTS? - "I am not a conformist. I am not concerned with the letters of man for I am He which has come that they be unbound by their fetters. I say unto them which desireth the letter - unto them the letter.

I say unto thee: be ye as ones free from such bondage. I stand ready to free thee from thy bondage. Unto thee I say - give unto the letter no thought. <u>Hear</u> what I <u>say</u> for I shall say it in many ways as becomes me and serves mine purpose. I say I am no stranger in thine midst. While they know me not, I know them. I see them bowing down before the Golden Calf - and they worship at the shrines which they have set up. (Their own standards of education.) They guild them and bring unto them burnt offerings - yet they close me out.

Be ye not so foolish. <u>Be</u> <u>ye</u> <u>not</u> <u>so</u> <u>foolish</u>! I am come that ye might have Light - Wisdom - Freedom which is the Father's will. While the letter changeth and passeth away - and the letter is not the law - the letter is of no consequence other than to cause thee to see the "Word." The word is the power which shall provoke thine mind into action and thy mind shall be free from the letter. See what is meant within the Word, and let thine mind be staid on <u>me</u> - the Light, the Way - Truth and Wisdom."

"I am He which hast come - that ye be free: forever free. I am Sananda - Son of God. Once known as the Nazarine, He which was born of Mary, Ward of Joseph.

Recorded by Thedra

Part - 2

THE WHITE BROTHERHOOD AND THE EMERALD CROSS.

THE MANY QUESTIONS ABOUT THE WHITE BROTHERHOOD AND THE ORDER OF THE EMERALD CROSS MAY BE EXPLAINED IN A FEW SIMPLE WORDS.

ONE HAS TO EARN THE RIGHT TO BECOME A MEMBER - EITHER IN THIS LIFE OR OTHERS BEFORE OR AFTER - NONE ENTER UNPREPARED.

THE WHITE BROTHERHOOD - or - THE ROYAL ASSEMBLY is of the Realms of Light---not of Earth. The Ascended Masters have proven themself in the school of Earth (THE SCHOOL FOR GODS) who have trodden the path of INITIATION - overcome the trials and temptations of the mundane world - who have gained their freedom and ascended as the Lord Jesus Christ (Sananda). They have gone the ROYAL ROAD.

Knowing the path of the Initiate -- and its pitfalls -- and sorrow, they extend a hand in Fellowship - LOVE and WISDOM - NEVER depriving the candidate an opportunity to learn his lessons well -- for this is His salvation -- for this do they proffer their hand, NOT to do our part for us, but rather that we become strong and free by our own strength.

The Royal Assembly or the White Brotherhood have known all of the heartaches, the longing, crucifications, temptations and JOYS of the aspirant -- the candidate -- the Master -- the Sibor -- herein lies their strength, their understanding, their great love for us on the path.

Their love and understanding knows no bounds. They give help when necessary for our progress. They also withhold it wisely - should it deprive us of our lessons. The candidate on the path of initiation shall become self-responsible for all his actions -- all the energy allotted him throughout his whole EARTHLY existence - and make atonement for all his misused energy, for therein is his salvation.

There is no one else which will ever make this atonement for us (the candidate) on the path of unfoldment. While the host of "WHITE BROTHERS" Brothers of LIGHT are ready to assist, the candidate shall (MUST) put forth every effort to overcome all the forces of darkness which would deter his progress and earn for himself his freedom from BONDAGE.

THE EMERALD CROSS

THE EMERALD CROSS is a company – and an order of beings who work within the Brotherhood of MAN - and the Fatherhood of God - for the good of all mankind --- And at the head of this group is one known as MOTHER SARAH, the personification of love -- embodiment of all MOTHERS. That is: the LOVE of God made Manifest - in MOTHERS. The blessed Mother Sarah is the head of this Order of the Emerald Cross. And when one earns the Divine right and privileges to associate themselves with this Order, it is the joy of all the Orders - and Brothers of Light. I speak for the Order - for I am known as Merseda. (As told to Sister Thedra of the Order of the Emerald Cross).

COMANCHE - which is the porter at the door - which doth keep out the unworthy, the unjust, the unclean. The Door Keeper - the one responsible for the Temple Gate.

BITTER CUP - that which you would not like to partake of - that which poisons thee, that which is not good, that which torments thee - that which ye have given unto thy brother to torment him which returns unto thee as a boomerang to torment thee - which ye shall receive multiplied - which has accumulated in its swift flight. I say prepare not for thyself the bitter cup for ye shall drink of the portion which thou doth prepare for thy brother. Be ye not foolish - make it not bitter.

BLEST OF MINE BEING - I have given of Mine self that Mine beloved has being.

BLEST OF MINE PRESENCE - Have I not gone the long way? I have gone out from Mine place of abode that I might bring light unto the Earth that she might be lifted up - that the children thereof might be delivered of all bondage - that they might return unto the place from whence they went out. And have I not come unto thee many times that this be accomplished? Have I not done all which has been given unto me to do? Wherein have I failed thee? Have I not done all that I have come to do? - While it is not as yet finished, I shall not fail. My mission shall be finished ere I return unto Mine abiding place. Shall I not be unto the true and shall I not return the Victor?

GAVE OF HIMSELF - Did I not give of Mine Self - hast thou? Have I not been true unto Mine trust? Have I asked aught for Myself? Have I not done that which I have promised? Have I not given Mine All? Have I not come on a Sacrificial Mission? What more have I to give - other than myself?

PORE - The physical body - vehicle which thou dost use.

<u>INITIATION</u> - Thy preparation for the inner temple. Each step is an initiation. One step at a time - the overcoming of self - the world - the becoming that which I am.

<u>COSMOS</u> - That which is unseen throughout many universes by thy eyes. Great is the expanse of the Father's Kingdom and the total thereof is referred to as "throughout the Cosmos."

<u>LORD'S</u> <u>STRANGE</u> <u>ACT</u> - This I shall reveal in Mine own time.

<u>WALK</u> <u>WHICH</u> <u>WAY</u> <u>THY</u> <u>CROWN</u> <u>TILTS</u> <u>NOT</u> - as a Son of God. Do honor unto thy Father Mother God - and thou shall be as one which has the Royal Raiment upon thine shoulders - and ye shall wear it in honor and with dignity.

<u>WHEN</u> <u>IT</u> <u>SAYS</u> <u>IT</u> <u>IS</u> <u>RECORDED</u> - <u>WHEREIN</u> <u>IS</u> <u>IT</u> <u>RECORDED</u>? - In the secret place - in the eth - and within the inner temple - and wherein thou art are many things recorded - which I do speak of. Ye shall see these recordings when thou doth enter into the secret place of Mine abode. I say ye shall read the records wherein are written the records of all thy travels from the time ye left the Father Mother God until thine return unto him.

<u>WHAT</u> <u>IS</u> <u>MICHAEL'S</u> <u>FLAMING</u> <u>SWORD</u>? - "The "Sword of Truth and justice."

Recorded by Sister Thedra

Other Books by TNT Publishing

Who am I and Why Am I here?

The Significance of Existence

Death and the Incredible Life After

Fear of Death Removed

Paradise Regained

Spiritual Laws Revealed

Unseen Forces

Too Good to Be True

The Truth of Life in the Spirit World

He Who Has Ears

The Great Awakening, Volume I

The Great Awakening, Volume II

The Great Awakening, Volume III

The Great Awakening, Volume IV

The Great Awakening, Volume V

The Great Awakening, Volume VI

The Great Awakening, Volume VII

The Great Awakening, Volume VIII,
THE WHITE STAR OF THE EAST

The Great Awakening, Volume IX,
I THE LORD GOD SAY UNTO THEM

The Great Awakening, Volume X,
MINE INTERCOM MESSAGES FROM THE REALMS OF LIGHT

The Great Awakening, Volume XI,
THE BOOK OF THE LORD

The Great Awakening, Volume XII,
TEMPLE TEACHINGS FROM THE HIGHER REALMS

The Great Awakening, Volume XIII,
TEMPLE TEACHINGS FROM THE HIGHER REALMS

The Great Awakening, Volume XIV,
TEMPLE TEACHINGS FROM THE HIGHER REALMS

The Great Awakening, Volume XV,
TEMPLE TEACHINGS FROM THE HIGHER REALMS

Transfiguration Volume I

Transfiguration Volume II

Transfiguration Volume III

Transfiguration Volume IV

Transfiguration Volume V

Transfiguration Volume VI

Transfiguration Volume VII

Transfiguration Volume VIII

Contact us at

Email: goldtown11@gmail.com

Web: https://www.whoamiandwhyamihere.com/

www.ingramcontent.com/pod-product-compliance
Lightning Source LLC
LaVergne TN
LVHW051546070426
835507LV00021B/2427